Never Saying Goodbye

A Life Changing Road to Acceptance and Joy After the Loss of a Loved One

MARY JEAN TEACHMAN

ISBN: 0615954863
ISBN 13: 9780615954868

DEDICATED TO THE LOVING MEMORY OF:
RENATA MOORE

My intuitive advisor and spiritual Mother

TABLE OF CONTENTS

PART I -THE LOSS

PART II - HEALING . . . AND WHAT I LEARNED

ACKNOWLEDGEMENTS

When my son, Forrest, took his own life in 1995 I was devastated. I didn't know how I was going to continue. This is my story about how I survived and healed and learned to continue life without him. Slowly, I inched forward..a ray of light would shine for a moment and then disappear as quickly as it arrived. I was fortunate to have healers help me. Dr. John Upledger, Dr. George Goodheart and my precious intuitive counselor, Renata Moore, who brought me out of despair into happiness. She is one of the most important people in my life and I will always be eternally grateful to her. She is my spiritual mother. The idea of writing about my journey percolated for awhile. I had changed my purpose in life and my value system little by little and one day I realized my fruitful path had healed me.

I want to thank first, my husband, Gerry, who has helped me on my journey by always being loving and supporting - he spent hours reading my draft and giving me perfect advice. He is a doctor of philosophy and his insight has been invaluable. My full of love daughter, Valarie, who has stayed by my side. My stepsons, Robert and Jonathan and Carolyn, my daughter-in-law. My brothers, Tom, Jack, Kyle, who called me every day for 2 years after my son left this planet, and Jim. My sister-in-laws, Jan, Carol, Darlene and Maida. My spiritual sister, Liv Ullmann, for encouraging and guiding me from the beginning of writing my book. Donald Saunders, my nephew, who has always been a shoulder to lean on. My dear friend, Kathy Yaffe, for linking me up with my fabulous editor, Jill Kramer. My long time supportive, caring friend Barbara Yearn, who lost her daughter, Colbe, to bipolar disease. We spent countless hours on the phone consoling and helping one another. My Birthday Club, Phyllis, Lucia, Kathy, Beverly, Jeanne and Suzy. My yoga teachers, Carol in Fl; Barbara in NC and my acupuncture doctor, Mary in Florida. Lastly but not least, my dear, dear friends and they know who they are.

I am grateful to my parents for bringing me into this planet and for anyone who has helped me on this journey. The road of life has been covered with cutting stones but also soft green grass to walk on. I still have occasional stones to deal with but then the green grass soothes me.

PREFACE

A wall of water rose out of the ocean and slammed into the coastline. It came out of nowhere, surprising everyone. Many lives were changed. That's how tragedy hit me—like a wall of water. It knocked me down and enveloped me after the suicide of my son, Arthur Forrest Tull, II.

This is my story of the sorrows and joys that have made up my journey as I went from utter despair and hopelessness to hope. I floundered for the longest time. I found out how difficult it is to not want to get out of bed in the morning and to think I couldn't make it through even one more day. When this happened, I knew that life would never be the same, but I fought that change with every ounce of my being.

This is also my story of survival—coming back and going beyond where I'd been before. It is about what I did when my very foundation was pulled out from under me. I collapsed and then clawed back to get to even ground so I could stand again.

I can see now that's what I did, but it took me a few years to want to start clawing. However, claw I did, and then clawed again and again. I finally stood up and was able to continue on. I never imagined I could do it, but I did. Out of tragedy came my ability to walk the road to peace, joy, and happiness.

I hope that this book will help others claw back and find a life filled with joy, purpose, and beauty. I finally found peace and acceptance, and for that I am eternally grateful.

When Forrest left this planet (I don't use the word *died* because he did not), he shed his physical body and went back home where he came from. He had come to Earth to have a physical experience. It is my belief that we come back many times in different bodies, with the same soul, to experience all that we can. We have both male and female lives of poverty, wealth, joy, tragedy, subservience, disability, addiction, and illness. It's the only way to empathize with others. We gain true compassion and love as a result.

I understand that some people don't see life in the same way I do, and I respect that, but I believe that my soul is on this planet to learn valuable lessons. I've known Forrest in other lifetimes, I knew him in this one, and I will reunite with him again. We'll see what other work we have to do together. This makes a great deal of sense to me and is also very comforting.

I didn't write this book to sway anyone to my way of thinking . . . I'm just telling my story.

PART I
The Loss

CHAPTER 1

THE SUICIDE

The phone rang at 7:30 P.M., March 11, 1995. I heard my husband, Gerry, say, "Hello," then, "Oh no, oh no!"

I knew in that moment that my son, Forrest, had committed suicide. It had been a week since I'd heard from him. I'd called him, but he hadn't answered his phone. Forrest and I had always kept in close contact, talking by phone at least a couple times a week. When I didn't hear from him, my system went on alert. I knew that he had a tendency to be depressed. His whole thinking pattern would change from positive to negative, which frightened me due to his past history.

Concerned, I'd called my daughter, Valarie, that morning and asked, "Do you know if Forrest received the letter I sent to him earlier this week?" Forrest and I had had a disagreement the week before, and I didn't feel good about what had transpired, so I'd written him a letter to tell him how sorry I was. Forrest had always come to me when he had a problem, but I didn't realize how severe this one was.

Valarie told me, "I gave the letter to Dad to deliver to Forrest. I'll call him and see if he did that." (My ex-husband lived near Forrest's home.) She called back and said, "Dad and Forrest had coffee a few days ago, and when they were leaving, he turned to Dad and said, "I need my freedom. You understand that, don't you?"

Alarms went off in my head when I heard that. Just a few words, but enough to set my heart racing with fear. Something was wrong. "Call your father immediately," I told Valarie. "Have him send someone to your brother's place to see if he's okay."

And then, nervous and edgy, I waited for the phone call. When it came, I knew what the news would be: my son was gone. I knew, and yet a part of my brain refused to accept it. My husband hung up the phone and tried to tell me, but I just kept walking around the living room saying, "Don't tell me. It's not true. Don't tell me. It's not true."

I was incapable of accepting the truth. It would crush me to let the reality in. It was as if I were in another dimension where the truth couldn't reach me. It was the most devastating day of my life. My entire life changed. A mother's worst nightmare became a reality for me. My wonderful and much-loved son, Arthur Forrest Tull, II, had taken his life with a gun.

Nothing made sense anymore. This couldn't be possible. My brain couldn't comprehend it. Why had this happened? What had I done to cause it? Please tell me this isn't true. My son has to still be alive! It was incomprehensible to me that my son had taken his own life with a gun. What had driven him to do that? What were his last thoughts?

This was a nightmare happening while I was awake. "Please tell me this is all a mistake," I said out loud. All I could do was wail most of that night. I got in and out of bed, in and out of the bathtub, and paced the floor—anything to establish some sense of normalcy so the piercing pain would dissipate. Sometime around 2:30 a.m., it did release me, just for a moment. I was getting back into bed when, all of a sudden, a beautiful wave of love encompassed me. Somewhere inside of me, I knew it wasn't from here, and I was in bliss for one second—an all-too-brief, momentary reprieve—and then the agony returned.

I'd never gone through such a devastating and frightening night. My emotions hit rock bottom, and I ached all over. I'll never know how I got through that night. I couldn't sleep, and my mind was filled with torment. It seemed as if I were a shell of a person and would never be anything but that. My anguish was unbearable.

As the night wore on, the reality of what had happened finally began to set in, and I went deeper and deeper into sorrow. I had nothing left. By morning I was in a zombie-like state. I was so absorbed in my own agony that I couldn't think about what Valarie, my beautiful daughter, was going through and the loss she was experiencing. All I could think was, my son is gone, and I will never see him again.

I clung to Gerry. I was in such shock that I didn't want to let reality in. I kept saying to him, "This can't be happening." But it was. Dawn came, and we flew from Florida to our house in Michigan. Forrest had lived in Michigan, also. There was no word that a note from Forrest had been found. If only there were some words from him explaining why this had happened. My last conversation with Forrest hadn't been the best. He'd had a request, and I'd turned him down. Now my decision haunted me. I was sure that my refusal was the reason he'd taken his life. My mind never rested for a moment. I just kept questioning, "Why, why?" I had never experienced such emotional devastation.

Then it was 5:30 that evening. I was in our bedroom, when suddenly the same beautiful wave of love I'd felt the night before enveloped me. At that exact moment, Valarie came into the room with a letter in her hand—a letter Forrest had written to us. I grabbed it eagerly and, while touching it, realized that this paper had been in Forrest's hand.

Dear Mom, Dad and Val,

My death was an intentional drug overdose, not a relapse. I believed narcotics the easiest way out. I repeat: I did not relapse. I had virtually no future, no reason to live, I can't even drive my car and I don't know the world of 1995. From 1984 to 1991, I lived in a haze in the drug culture, not being in touch with the "progress of the world." Then, until a few months ago I hid from the world in AA. Now I find that I am not equipped to survive in 95 because my world exists only back in the early 80s. My head cleared up and I cannot handle 1995. Things seem so strange to me. I apologize for this. Don't cry for me for I am in heaven and just fine.

Please do not bury my body. Cremate it and scatter my ashes on Woodward Avenue going south between 13 1/2 and 13 mile. I owe Big Jim $500 and I would be thankful if you would pay him for me. It would be best if it were not made public that I used narcotics, for the sake of the kids in AA. Again, I have no real future, my body is still wasted from all of the drugs and my legs are so weak I have a hard time walking. I have near fatal cardiovascular conditioning and I can't quit smoking. In all, I have a better future in heaven and I'm not the least bit afraid to die, it's what I want and I hope some day you'll understand. I love you all and I ask you to try to understand that this was best.

Love,
Forrest

In his own way and as logically as possible, my son was trying to tell us why he'd left. It was clear from what he'd written that he saw no future here on Earth and that leaving would be a welcome release. His reiteration was that this had not been a drug relapse—had he needed the drugs to be able to use the gun?

I reread the letter and then began to cry. My heart was broken, and I didn't think it would ever heal. My son had found his freedom from pain, but my own hell was just beginning.

* * *

Gerry took care of all the arrangements for the memorial service, since I wasn't capable of handling anything. Per his request, Forrest was cremated immediately, and his ashes were at the service. I was touched by the number of people who came to pay their respects. My son had been part of the drug culture but had been clean for four years. I was especially grateful to the young people who attended—he'd counseled them one-on-one and at rehab centers. They were from all walks of life, some with tattoos and piercings on their bodies, others in business suits.

Forrest had been able to connect with them because he'd taken drugs himself. He understood what they were going through. They could relate to each other, as the drugs formed a common bond, a shared experience.

And now there was one more common denominator that united those who were left: they loved Forrest and mourned his loss. Some were so devastated that all they could say was: "He saved my life. Why couldn't he save his own?"

One by one, each approached me and told me what Forrest had meant to them and how he'd helped them. I could feel their grief and loss as they embraced me, and in some strange way, I was taken out of my pain for a short time. My eyes took them in, my heart reached out to theirs, and I could feel a connection to my son through them.

These friends of Forrest's will never know what comfort they provided me. More than just a blanket of love, they gave me a confirmation of what Forrest had been committed to over the past four years. They validated his existence as they mourned his departure.

Then, everyone sat down and the ceremony began. The minister said a few kind words, and then Gerry got up and read a note that Forrest had left for me several years previously—a note that perfectly captured his sense of humor:

> Mom,
>
> I know that you will be busy today, but if you get a chance could you please pick up some Minute Maid orange juice and chicken. I would also like a New York strip from the gourmet counter at Great Scott. Also, if you could pick up a Ferrari 308 GTS and a Rolex watch along with a jet powered helicopter, I would be very thankful. But I really just need the orange juice, at least. Because if I wake up and do not have any orange juice, I may go on a rampage, and redecorating the entire lower level and rebuilding most of the upper would be a hassle and more expensive than just getting some orange juice anyway. So for all of us to be happy, it would be a simple matter to get me some Minute Maid orange juice.
>
> I was really just joking about the Ferrari and the Rolex and the helicopter, I don't want you to really get me those things. I know that they cost a lot of money but

> maybe a Corvette would be nice or even just a Citation. Hell, at this point, not owning a car, I would settle for an old horse and a small cart. But I really need the orange juice. There was just a new study released from the authorities that says that a son given orange juice will live longer than a son who had to drink water and eat beans. So you want to be real careful and do just what they say so that you do not disrupt the balance of nature.
>
> I don't really want an old plow horse and a cart or anything, I was just joking. But maybe a little pushcart that I could push to work, heck, I'll take a skateboard at this point. But I really want the orange juice . . . eggs too.

I told Gerry that, if I could, I wanted to read a poem that Forrest had written about my mother, who was no longer with us, because he'd had a deep love for her. It was very important to me to read that poem because I wanted everyone to have another glimpse of Forrest and who he was.

After the minister read a brief biography of Forrest, I stood up, walked to the podium with every ounce of strength that I had, and put the poem down on the polished surface. I grabbed the sides of the stand to steady me. I proceeded to read, wavering a few times but successfully reaching the end. Afterward, I looked at my son's ashes and said, "I'm proud of you, my son, and I love you very much."

I wanted everyone to know that even though he'd left in an unconventional way, that did not diminish his life.

Once the service was over, there was an informal get-together at the local coffeehouse where Forrest used to read his poetry. People talked and laughed, remembering him and sharing stories about his life. Gradually, however, they began to leave, returning to their lives, leaving me to find a new life—one that no longer included my son.

* * *

CHAPTER 2

AFTER THE MEMORIAL

After the memorial, the hardest days of my life unfolded before me. Every morning I asked myself, "How can I get through this day?" Every thought found its way back to Forrest. At first I could only think about my role in all of this. I told Gerry, "Surely I was the culprit who caused this terrible tragedy."

He immediately said, "No, no! There's no way that's true," but I wasn't convinced. I was in a fog. My family and friends kept me going.

I would get up each morning and think, I cannot get through one more day. I know, I'll call Forrest. Then reality would hit. He wasn't here anymore. I just wanted to put my head under the covers and never come out. I didn't know how to cope. I knew that my family and friends were also suffering the loss, but I was only able to think of myself and my pain. I also thought of Forrest's bipolar ailment and the role that had played in all of this.

Prior to Forrest's death, I was hanging on to the hope that there would be a cure for his disease. Now that he was gone, I had no hope. I felt like I was walking on the edge of a steep mountain with a deep gorge below, and at any moment I could step off and fall to my death. I told myself, "Don't slip."

Despair and sadness were my friends, and that's all I wanted. People would ask me, "How are you doing?" But I was unable to answer as huge tears fell from my eyes and splashed onto my cheeks.

The sadness never left me. It hung over me like a shroud. From that moment on, I looked at life from a different perspective. I had two philosophies that I'd always lived by:

1. You can do it if you want to.
2. When there's life, there's hope.

But neither had any value anymore. Forrest couldn't do it, even if he wanted to. He couldn't continue to live his life because it was too painful. And there was no more life, so how could I hope?

I told myself, "If only I could have seen this coming, I would have been able to stop it." I always thought the love of a mother makes the impossible, possible, but my power as a mother had proven to be limited, if it had been there at all; and that was the hardest thing for me to accept. My love was abundant, but it hadn't been enough. I never imagined I was going to lose a child. I'd been given this precious being and took for granted that I would see him through his life journey—with me going first, not him. I never imagined that the end of his life would come about as it had.

At first, I held my son's photo—the one that was used for the memorial—tightly in my hand. I constantly kissed it. Seeing Forrest's face consoled me. On the back of the picture was an excerpt from a letter that he'd written to his stepfather and me:

> While under the pressure of coping with society, it is often difficult to really be aware how great many things are. I feel so lucky now that I can look at what we have and appreciate it. I am so proud to be a part of this family and I love you all. I often do not express my true feeling verbally because I find it difficult. But you can all be assured I love you and am thankful you are part of my life.

The trauma of the shock kept me going in and out of reality. I knew what had happened but wished desperately that it had not. Everyone went back to their lives, as it should be, and I had more time to think. The thinking was a killer. The more I thought, the worse it became. There didn't seem to be a way out.

I remembered some of our times together, especially birthdays and holidays. Thanksgiving was the hardest for me because that was the last time I'd seen Forrest. He'd enjoyed dinner with the family—Gerry had cooked because I'd been ill in bed. After dinner, he came into the bedroom to say good-bye. Little did I know that that was the last time we would be together.

That memory is etched into my mind. Forrest had been so tender and caring. I can still see his tall, lithe body sitting next to me. He held my hand and we had a wonderful talk. He turned to me and said, "I love you, Mom."

I answered, "I love you too, Forrest." I remember looking into his large, compassionate eyes and feeling a very strong energy between us. It was a moment I will cherish forever.

As I recalled that feeling, I was momentarily at peace. Then the guilt returned. I kept thinking that if I'd done something different, the suicide wouldn't have occurred. Friends and therapists could tell me that it wasn't my fault until they were blue in the face, but I didn't believe them! How could I? I knew better. After all, I was his mother and I knew. Mother knows best.

All I could do was mourn, and I felt as if I'd been hit by a train. I realized that life would never be the same again. The thought ran through my mind that that maybe I should commit suicide, but I knew I couldn't do that to my family. Not only that, but the thought terrified me.

I didn't want to see anyone. I'd never experienced emotions like this before. Every day I had to fight an emotional battle, and the sorrow was relentless. The days and nights were endless. I'd been told that the pain would abate in time, but I wondered how much time it would take. I questioned my strength. It seemed to be leaving me, and I didn't know how to get it back. People can take certain foods and vitamins or lift weights to make the body strong, but what helps the emotions and mind overcome such a loss? Nothing seemed to be able to reach inside and shore me up. I had to find a way. I was confused. I just didn't know what to do, or where or whom to turn to. Life was a maze, and I couldn't find my way out.

I truly believed I would never smile again. A close friend asked me, "Are you ever going to be happy again?" I had no answer for her. I was just so closed off from happiness. Each moment awake reminded me that Forrest was gone. I would never again see him walk into the house, say, "Hi, Mom," and put his comforting arms around me. We would never again have our interesting and wonderful talks.

My husband was so understanding, He'd wrap his arms around me and support me completely. It helped, but it wasn't enough.

* * *

I believe that things happen for a reason, that there are lessons to be learned. But how could I find out what this lesson held for me? I felt so lonely. Where could I turn? Would my lingering sadness ever leave? I felt as though I'd been ripped apart, as if something had cut into me and pulled out a vital organ. I couldn't operate without it. How could I put the pieces back together if a vital part was gone? I had no answer.

My son's apartment was cleaned out by a special crew that handles those situations, and I was given the few items he owned. He'd given most of his possessions away before he left. I held the remaining ones and cherished them. I put them in a box in a spare bedroom in my home so I could take them out and hold them. They consoled me. I hung Forrest's coat in our front closet, and I'd look at it and touch it almost every day. After all, he'd worn it many times, and his smell was on it. Those moments when I handled his clothing made me feel closer to him. No one would have been able to wrest those items away from me.

Gerry and I love to go to the movies, so one month after Forrest's death we went, looking forward to being distracted for a few hours. We got our popcorn and settled down in our seats. I was enjoying the film when all of a sudden an actor in the film pulled out a gun, put it to his head, and shot himself. I gasped and hid my head in my lap when I saw the gun going to the man's head. I was in a panic. It brought me right back to Forrest. I was as vulnerable as the day he'd left. I couldn't stand it. I got sick and had to leave. I grabbed Gerry and said, "I have to go, I have to go now!"

Gerry jumped up and said, "Yes, yes, now." We ran out of the theater. The scene lingered in my head. We'd tried to escape our pain by going out for a few hours of entertainment and experienced a traumatic occurrence.

I thought, Will the torment never leave? Will incidents like this happen again and again and haunt me forever?

I looked for books that could help me during my time of grief and performed everyday chores to occupy my time. My only goal was to get through the day, then another day, then another day, until a week, and then a month, had passed. Some days it seemed like a bolt of lightning would hit me and the wound would be wide open again. There was so much unrelenting pain in not being with Forrest; the void was huge, and only he could fill it.

I would say to Gerry, "If only I could see him for one minute, that would suffice."

I knew that was impossible, but just thinking of that possibility seemed to help in some strange way.

It is said that time heals all wounds. I believed that was true, so I knew I had to put some salve on the wound. But what salve could I use? I looked in the medicine cabinet to find the right one. Maybe I could find the right ointment for my emotions and my brain. I knew I had to keep looking. That awareness gave me hope for the first time. That's all I needed at that time: hope. Still, the sense of loneliness was overpowering. People were kind and compassionate, but I knew no one could alleviate my pain. If I couldn't do it, how could they?

* * *

But a friend did end up helping. About two months after Forrest's death, she told me about suicide groups that helped people like me. I called a couple of hospitals and found one. Gerry, Valarie, and I attended our first meeting together. I was moved by being with people who understood what we were going through. I heard their stories and got out of my own malaise momentarily. Valarie and I continued to go for about three months. We identified with the other mothers, sisters, brothers, sons, and daughters whose hearts were aching like ours. We saw that we weren't alone. These people were also just trying to get by, day by day.

There were 15 men and women in our group. All of their stories touched me deeply, but particularly one mother's story.

She said, "I was preparing dinner one evening when I heard a shot from the basement. I quickly ran downstairs and found my son on the basement floor, dead of a gunshot wound. I screamed with agony." She paused and continued, "He was 15 years old. I had no idea what had been going on inside my son's brain. He seemed like a normal teenager, not one with problems to cause him to do that."

I could feel this woman's pain. It struck me how much worse it was for her to see the actual result of her son's suicide. I was spared that. If I hadn't been, I don't think I would have ever gotten that image out of my mind.

I confessed to the group, "I can't let go. I just can't let go. I've tried to let go the guilt, but I just can't do it."

Members of the group told me, "Forrest would have taken his life no matter what you'd done." I didn't believe them.

When they said, "It was nothing you did or didn't do," it didn't make sense to me. I could listen to their rationale, but it didn't ring true for me. It was as though I was holding on to something because then I still had a connection to Forrest. If I took any of it away by telling myself I should have done something—or many things—differently, then I was taking a piece of our life together and negating it. It's all I had. I could take the pain—maybe that was my punishment. I felt I certainly deserved it.

One of the main advantages of being among those who have the same experience is that we're able to openly cry with unabashed emotion. We wept as though it were a natural event, and no one felt uncomfortable. There was such love and compassion in that room. That was my first step toward healing.

* * *

I really said good-bye to Forrest when Gerry and Valarie and I scattered his ashes on his birthday, August 30, 1995. We asked relatives and some of his friends to join us in the ritual. When Forrest was in his late teens, he'd raced cars on a main street in Royal Oak, Michigan, and that was where he wanted his ashes to be released. He was very clear in his note as to how that should be done, so we followed his instructions to the letter.

It was a warm, clear night with just a slight breeze in the air when we went to Woodward Avenue, between 13 and 13-1/2 Mile Road where he used to race. We waited until the sun set and then stood in the median with cars racing by. It was mystical and emotional for all of us. We each took a scoop, lifted our arms, and let the wind from the speeding cars carry Forrest's ashes aloft into the atmosphere. I was the last person to participate. I was hesitant for a moment and then, with love, threw up my arms and released him to the universe. At that exact moment, a red Mustang pulled up beside us, stopped for a second, revved up its engine, and raced off down Woodward.

We all exclaimed excitedly, "Look, look! Forrest is telling us that he's with us." A perfect ending to a heartrending evening. I still have the small container with my son's ashes on my desk. They comfort me in the most wonderful way.

I wrote heartfelt letters to Forrest during this period:

June 1, 1995
Dear Forrest,

The days are still dismal with more patches of sunshine. I miss you so desperately. I'm sorry I didn't understand your disease more. I will always remember your days on earth and cherish them. I don't resent you for taking your own life. Life here was too painful for you. In the deepest part of my mind, I feel I cannot go on but I know I must. I become a little frightened when I think you are gone

and recognize that I fear I cannot handle it. I don't want to feel sorry for myself, just love for you. Why is it that I couldn't see into your soul until after you were gone? If only I could see you for one minute, that would help.
I love you.

Mom

July 27, 1995
Dear Forrest,

I am trying to get rid of the guilt. I keep going over all the times I could have handled things differently but it is not doing any good. I have lost my self confidence. I'm beating myself into the ground and making myself sick. I was trying to help but I don't think I did. I am sorry for that. I ask your forgiveness. I long to hold you and tell you how much I love you, always have and always will. Love is the important issue, not guilt. I send you love and light.

Mom

August 14, 1995
Dear Forrest,

I am experiencing a most profound, agonizing loss of you. Your dear, exquisite, bright face is before me often. I never want to lose seeing you. I see you at all stages of your life and I cherish them all. I only remember the wonderful times we had together because that is all I want to. I really had no appreciation of how lucky I was to be your mother. In my heart you are still my little boy and I wish you still were then I could do so many things differently. I would foster your individuality and try to help you more with your devastating disease. I feel I let you down. I realize now how much you loved me and how you needed my love and understanding. I know I have to completely come to terms with your suicide and I know I will when the time is right. You reside in my heart. I love you, my son, with my very being.

Mom

September 9, 1995
Dear Forrest,

You are such a good, kind soul and I must remember your earthly personality got in your way. You couldn't figure life out. You are a shining beacon to me. I am trying to get over my guilt. I still wish I could have helped you more. I was incredibly ignorant. I should not have left any stone unturned. I must and will help others so they don't have to go through what you went through. Releasing your ashes on your birthday gave you and me a freedom, me because I know I released you from this earthly plane. Your life's journey is more and more evident to me. I'm sorry that you had so much pain.

Love,
Mom

I knew I had to take even more steps to heal. There was a hole in my heart, but I hoped that I could fill the hole with love and then Forrest would continue to be a part of me. It would probably take a long time, but I knew I had to find a way.

* * *

CHAPTER 3

FORREST'S LIFE

I decided to look back over Forrest's life and try to figure out why he'd committed suicide. By going back, I thought I might be able to move forward.

* * *

One of the most powerful experiences in my life was Forrest's birth. That precious little baby awakened profound love in me. Forrest was an interesting being from the time he was born. A couple of hours after he arrived, the nurse carried him to me and was astonished by how alert and strong he was. He acted as if he was able to see what was going on. He came in on Labor Day and was ready for action.

That's the advantage and disadvantage of being a mother. I saw so much potential in him from the beginning, and then, in later life, saw him struggling and trying to hang on. He became ill shortly after birth, and the doctor said, "Your son is allergic to milk. Boil down a gallon of milk to eight ounces and give it to him."

But Forrest didn't react favorably, so the doctor then suggested, "Give him a soy milk product," and that didn't work either. I was in a panic. The doctor advised trying still another soy product, and it worked! Success! The first crisis of my son's life was over.

Forrest was a loving, bright boy. When he started talking, it was in complete sentences. I remember when he was four, he looked up at me and said, "Mommy, I love you so much. I want to be back in your tummy."

Yes, there was a spiritual bond between us. He would go outside to play (we didn't have a fence), and I would tell him, "Don't ever leave the yard."

He answered "I won't, Mommy."

I said, "You promise?

And he replied, "I do." I knew it was written in stone. He would keep his promise.

I got divorced when Forrest was in third grade, and we moved to another school district. It was very difficult for him, so I took him to a counselor to be evaluated, and the diagnosis was benign. In fact, his early life didn't raise any alarms about what he was about to experience in his teens.

I remarried in 1971. Forrest and Valarie loved their stepfather, Mort Lieberman, and called him "Pop." At the time, Forrest was about to enter high school, but the school district we were in wasn't good, so we sent him to private school close to home. We applied late, and the only way he could get in was to board. That wasn't a good decision on our part, as he was put in a dorm with older boys. I didn't realize anything was wrong until I got a disturbing call early one morning three months after he started school. I was told, "Forrest is in the school infirmary. We don't know exactly what's wrong with him. Please come and pick him up." I hung up the phone and immediately rushed there with great apprehension.

Forrest was acting terrified when I arrived and said, "Mom, I can't go back to my room—it terrifies me."

I tried to find out what had terrified him, but I never could. I couldn't get a definitive answer from the school, either. They handed me a piece of paper with a psychiatrist's number on it and said, "Please call him; he can give you some answers."

Basically, Forrest went to bed in a normal state and then woke up in the middle of the night experiencing what he never had before, and we had no idea what that was. His life changed, and so did ours. I should have dug deeper, but that's all in retrospect.

We immediately took Forrest to the psychiatrist, but he didn't have a diagnosis. I realize now that he didn't know. The insidious grasp of mental disease had started to take hold. It was the beginning of many torturous days and nights for Forrest and our entire family. The worst part was that he was misdiagnosed and was put on the wrong medication. And we couldn't seem to help.

One thing I do know now is that this was the onset of Forrest's bipolar symptoms. They were starting to rear their ugly head. Very little was known about the bipolar condition, called manic depression at that time. We did what we thought would help, but we didn't really know what was wrong. No one during those first turbulent, confusing years could give us a diagnosis.

We didn't know what was happening and didn't know what to do. I've always been viewed as a strong person, but little did anyone know that I was falling apart on the inside. My early training came in handy. I was taught: "It's how one perceives you on the outside that's important." I kept repeating that mantra to myself. It was as though I had two lives: one that other people saw, and one that I knew about. My stomach was in knots a great deal of the time.

Forrest developed fears that had never surfaced before. He'd say, "Mom, my mind races all the time and I can't stop it." I can't imagine being in a situation where your mind is racing all the time and you're feeling utter confusion, on top of being misdiagnosed and being put on the wrong medication.

I put all my faith in the doctors, and I'm sure they were doing the best they could. Not surprisingly, Forrest's interest in school subjects waned. When he was four years old, he was tested; and he scored in the 99th percentile in his age group, so he was obviously highly intelligent, but this wasn't reflected in his grades.

He also acquired a love of racing dirt bikes, and I suppose the sense of danger excited him. He had long hair, which was fairly unusual for that time, but he seemed to enjoy being different. In school, the main subject he became dedicated to was film—he always got A's in that class.

The long, hard years began for Forrest and our family. He was incredibly bright, talented, unique, good-looking, kind, and fun to have around—he had a great sense of humor. So how could he be ill? I now know that this happened because Forrest inherited the bipolar gene. I also know that it can appear one day and simply take up residence. Forrest didn't exhibit bizarre behavior; he seemed to be in sync with other teenage boys. But something was clearly wrong.

Forrest did finish high school, and he attended a community college for a short time, but then quit and worked at a variety of small jobs. He didn't have any direction and consequently had no idea what he wanted to do. Racing cars on Woodward in Birmingham, Michigan, was a popular thing to do back then; and Forrest loved it.

At that time, he met a man who was an executive and who also loved to race. This gentleman asked him why he wasn't in college and why was he wasting his time when he obviously was smart enough to get a degree. After many conversations, this man convinced Forrest to go to Northwood College. He applied and got in.

My son did well in his studies and appeared to be mentally and physically healthy. He didn't drink or smoke and wasn't depressed. In fact, he was off medication for two years. He also took up weightlifting and ate well. There was a lull in his disease, but it was waiting in the wings to reappear—bipolar disease can fool you.

Forrest got a two-year degree, and his life seemed to be going well. He had many friends—he'd always had a lot of friends. After he graduated, his friends had a party twice a month, and it would be scheduled around a letter that Forrest would write and send to them. All of the students marveled over the content. Unfortunately, I don't have any copies. But they do reveal another component of his personality. We thought that maybe the storm was over. How wrong we were.

* * *

Forrest decided to go to another college with the goal of getting a Ph.D. in philosophy and eventually becoming a professor at a small college. He came from a long line of educators: his paternal grandfather had been a teacher who'd founded the Detroit Business Institute and other business schools. It seemed like a good choice for Forrest. He did incredibly well in his philosophy classes, but during the last quarter, he suddenly quit school. He seemed to lose his direction in life.

Sufferers of mental illnesses aren't responsible for their diseases any more than someone with an inherited heart disease or genetic diabetes. In that respect, Forrest was a victim. He didn't ask for this disease; he was stricken with it. He was tagged genetically from both sides of the family. If someone is ill with cancer or has a broken arm or any other ailment, people are sympathetic, but it's not the same with mental illness. People don't necessarily show understanding or compassion. They expect sufferers to react to life in the same way as someone who's normal.

Sufferers try to hide mental diseases because they know how others will react. But they shouldn't have to feel ashamed about being sick. Entire families are affected by these diseases, but aren't suffering to the same degree that the sufferers are. That's why we need to gain a better understanding of mental illness. I don't know how I would have lived my life if I'd been stricken with bipolar disorder.

I must admit that I tried to hide Forrest's behavior from family and friends. I didn't completely understand this insidious disease at the time. I now know that it's a brain disease caused by a chemical reaction in the body. If you took away insulin from a diabetic and told him to run a ten-mile marathon, he could die. It's not any different for someone with bipolar disorder. Medication is a must. If medicine isn't given to sufferers of mental disease, they have great difficulty dealing with their lives, and some die. Many homeless people suffer from mental illness.

Forrest had never planned on having children because he didn't want to pass the disease on to them. Also, a couple romantic relationships ended because of his decision. He was thinking beyond himself. He would say to me, "Mom, I would never pass this disease on to anyone." I thought that was so brave and admirable.

My son fought a valiant battle with bipolar disorder for 23 years, but he couldn't continue fighting every day. Nobody could tell that Forrest was fighting a losing battle because he appeared other than he was. He used to say to me, "Mom, people can't see how difficult life is for me because there's nothing physically wrong." He looked fine on the outside but was broken on the inside. There were periods in his life when the torment subsided, but those times grew fewer as he got older.

Forrest was hospitalized four times. Following is a poem he wrote while he was in a mental facility. The horror screams out.

My First Night In The Nuthouse

Bloodcurdling screams of extreme pain and horror penetrated the thick hospital air. The ward was teaming with the frustrations and anxieties of many people in mental agony calling out into the night for help

"I want to go home," cried a shrill voice

People in dirty pajamas and slippers shuffled up and down the halls trying to make sense of what was happening to them.

"I want to go home!" screamed a shrill and ear-piercing voice that trailed off into the night

Small and uncomfortable beds in cramped and cold rooms made for an impossible situation in which to sleep

"GOD, PLEASE LET ME GO HOME!!!"

Bloodshot eyes and slurred speech, certain evidence of troubled souls

It was nearly midnight and the nuthouse was as active as Vegas at noon

Nervous and upset people searching each other's souls for answers that don't exist anywhere

A hopeless prison term to be served by one and all whether in or out of the ward. Prisoners to sick minds, troubled and poisoned, confused and misguided, tired and angry

"We all want to go home!"

> Looking through the thick shatterproof windows, we could see the activities of the world outside
>
> What a thin line that divides those on the outside from the in
>
> Helpless and frightened people with nowhere to turn. No place to hide from the ever present insanity
>
> Even the medication cannot help us now
>
> We are spending the first of many nights in the nuthouse

These were dark hours that I wasn't a part of. Forrest was going through his life with a mental disease and a drug addiction. The disease led him to drugs, and he was powerless over them. So was I. I tried to help by sending him to various facilities and doctors and by being there for him, but the power of the disease was too much for him. The disease ate away at my son until he was so tired that there didn't seem to be any other way out.

Sleep can be so restoring to the body and mind, and it's the first defense against bipolar disorder. If Forrest didn't sleep, mania was waiting to strike. But he had great trouble sleeping and would write poetry during those long nights. There's a sense of loneliness when one is awake and everyone else is asleep. Life doesn't look the same. More neuroses and anxieties come forth.

Forrest took medicine to sleep, but he said it robbed him of his creativity. What a dilemma! He wanted to write into the night, but if he took sleep medication, he couldn't write. He solved this problem by being awake until the wee hours of the morning and sleeping through part of the day. He took night jobs such as a security guard in order to deal with his issues.

* * *

CHAPTER 4

BIPOLAR AND DRUGS

There had been some hard times before, but nothing like what was about to occur. Drugs were about to enter Forrest's life. I don't know the exact date he got involved with them, but I have a suspicion he smoked pot with some older boys on his last night in the dorm of high school. It seems the parents are the last to know. It was part of that era of thinking that drugs aren't harmful or addictive.

Forrest and I had discussions about that, and we completely disagreed. I told him, "They are addictive and harmful."

He replied, "No, they aren't."

He started living with a girl who was on cocaine, and I pleaded. "Forrest, please don't live with her because the odds are high that you'll start taking cocaine, too." Well, he did live with her and did take cocaine. That was the true beginning of his downward spiral.

I understand now that many bipolar individuals take drugs or alcohol in order to self-medicate. They're attacked every day by the disease and simply want relief. So Forrest was now going through his life with a mental disease and an addiction and I wasn't able to help. Of course I tried, by sending him to various facilities and doctors and by being there for him, but the strength of the disease was too much for him. It ate away at him until he was so tired that he was no longer able to resist the drug culture.

Forrest did drugs for about ten years, but he was clever and fooled us. Initially we didn't think he was on drugs. But during those ten years, the combination of the drugs, the disease, and my lack of knowledge as far as how to deal with my son's issues caused us to have many serious conflicts. I feel that if I'd had the knowledge about bipolar disorder that I now have, I would have handled the situation differently and possibly, just possibly, he would be here today.

Forrest fought for years and was tired. The strength just left him. Depression crept in and haunted him, and was always around the corner waiting to strike.

The downward spiral continued, and Forrest eventually became hooked on heroin. At times, he couldn't separate reality from delusion. He went into the worst part of town to satisfy his habit, but I didn't know all this was going on while it was happening. He lived away from home, so I didn't see him at his worst. When I think about it now, I probably had my own form of delusion going on. I was guilty of not truly looking at what was occurring.

For example, Forrest got involved in car accidents where the police would stop him, supposedly for no reason. He hung around with troubled people and was unrealistic and didn't have any direction. I had a desperate need to believe everything he told me because that would prevent me from looking at the reality of the situation. It was impossible for me to think that Forrest was on hard drugs. But he was.

I don't know all the grim details of his life at that time, but I do know that his fiancée died of a drug overdose while he was sleeping soundly in the same room, not aware what was happening because he was high himself. He woke up to find her dead on the floor. He was riddled with guilt and heartbroken. He told me, "Mom, I loved her so much. I can't sleep because all I do is think of her."

But I was seething with anger and blamed him. I couldn't sympathize with his loss. I could only think about the fact that he took drugs and caused the ultimate pain to her and her family. I tried to get all of those thoughts out of my mind, but it took a long time for me to forgive him.

Just recently, I found out that Forrest called his cousin Bill to help him out at one time. It was four years after the death of his girlfriend. He asked Bill, "Could you drive me over to Laura's parents' home? I have to ask for their forgiveness." They were devastated and held Forrest responsible for her death.

Forrest explained, "I don't know if they'll close the door in my face, but this is something I have to do." He had recovered from drugs temporarily and wanted, in some way to right a wrong, if he could.

So Bill drove him over there, and Forrest anxiously went to the door, knocked hesitantly, and waited for it to open. Her parents appeared, immediately embraced him, and invited him in. He talked to them for about an hour and a half. I don't know the conversation that took place, but it was certainly cleansing for Forrest and apparently for them. His cousin also told me that Forrest cried nonstop for about an hour after he got back into the car. He pleaded, "Bill, Please, just drive around for a while."

It pains me that I didn't know any of this and couldn't do anything about the agony that my son was going through. I cry as I write this.

* * *

My late husband, Mort Lieberman, stepfather of Forrest and Valarie, was dying of cancer around this time. He had the disease for eight years and fought it valiantly. He was in the hospital for the last six weeks of his life and passed away on March 2, 1989. Forrest was still on drugs, taking methadone.

During the funeral, it was evident to us that he needed help. My brothers, Tom and Kyle, and I tried to find a dual diagnostic facility for him to go to. At that time, there were primarily rehab facilities that didn't allow any medication for any illness. We did find one that was located in Detroit, and it was mandatory that he stay for at least three days.

I got a call from Forrest on the fourth day about 8 o'clock on a dark, windy night. He told me, "I left the hospital. I'm standing on a street corner in a very rough part of Detroit with nowhere to go." I was furious that he'd left, but knew that I had to pick him up. The thought of him being in that part of town terrified me.

I said, "Tell me exactly where you are, and I'll pick you up, but you can't stay at the house." We had an agreement that he could never stay at our home again if he was on drugs. I drove to get him with my heart beating rapidly all the way. I picked him up and drove him to a small motel far away from stores and restaurants.

I said, "I'll bring you food and come spend the day with you, but I'm not giving you any money. You can call me if you need anything."

I was trying to get him into the Menninger Clinic in Kansas, so I talked to a doctor at that facility. I told him everything that had happened. He was sympathetic, called back, and told me, "I got Forrest a bed." My son stayed there for about three months, and when he came back to Michigan, it was the first time that he tried desperately to get clean.

Forrest was going to a methadone clinic to get his weekly dose. The man who ran the clinic asked him, "Why are you doing this?"

Forrest answered, "Because I can't stop."

The man replied, "I know how you can be helped." Forest was dubious. He got his dose and went home. But during that week, he thought about what the man had said.

The following week he went back to the clinic and asked the man, "How do I get off of drugs?"

The man told him, "Come to my church on Sunday, and when the pastor asks if there's anyone here with a problem, you stand up and tell him about yours. He will ask you what it is, and then you'll tell him."

Forrest went to the church the following Sunday morning (which was an African-American evangelical place of worship in the suburb of Pontiac), when the pastor asked if anyone in the congregation had a problem, Forrest stood up and said, "I have a problem."

The pastor asked, "What is the problem?"

Forrest said, "I can't get off drugs."

The parishioners immediately stood up and gathered around him and said, "You are not alone, we can help you. You can get through this."

The positive energy of love surrounded him, and an epiphany occurred. After that, he never took drugs again. He stopped cold, which was remarkable. I would say to Forrest, "What a wonderful thing you did," and he would say, "No, my higher power did this." I'm so proud that he got off drugs; it took so much strength and determination.

Forrest's complete recovery from drugs was unusual, and in a real sense almost miraculous. He turned his life around, joined Alcoholics Anonymous (AA), counseled young people, and was admired and loved by them. He had poems and a song written for him after he took his life, and people tell me that his influence is still felt today.

Forrest wrote the poem that follows. His dear friend Lisa Hook promised him she would publish it for him, which she did after he left the planet. It's raw and riveting, and it's difficult for me to read and feel the anguish he was going through. An addiction is powerful; it becomes number one.

Lisa introduced his poem with one she dedicated to him.

LOST IN THE FORREST

"The Life and Times of Forrest Tull"

by Lisa Buzko Hook

With gentle fierceness he spoke of light
Of a God that once guided him safely ashore
He wore black—he saw white
He sometimes spoke in tongues
He drew the young followers near
Enchanted by his tales
He was a miracle spared will from cruel fate's jaws
Slain his own merciless hand
He wore white—he saw black
His words were like magic
Spun from a far away land
Where people understood him
Without a whisper
Where he could find peace . . . black peace

Arthur Forrest Tull touched both the souls of countless people searching for salvation from the torment of addiction, and those seeking solace from the pain of mental illness.

Forrest was dedicated to guiding others toward the spiritual path that had been his saving grace from a life of heroin addiction. He also suffered from manic depressive illness, a demon which he fought on a daily basis. Yet he was the kind of person who would never turn his back on a friend in need—what was going on in your world was important to him and it showed. People were instantly drawn to his charismatic karma. Forrest once saved the life of a 19-year-old who was trying to hang himself. Tragically and ironically, however he took his own life. It was not heroin, but the demons in his head from manic depressive illness that he was unable to conquer, despite numerous hospitalizations, the support of an amazing family and a vast network of friends. He is loved and missed by all. He frequented coffee houses and read his poetry, because he had something remarkable to share. It was his wish that "Heroin The Omega" would reach those who would benefit from it's powerful message.

Lisa Buzko Hook

HEROIN THE OMEGA

I'm sittin' onna broken
Toilet
me
sittin onna broken toilet
filled with AIDS contaminated
human waste
from hookers n' junkies

me with
roaches
n'
condoms n'
filth
at my feet
from
a hundred million
pathetic
fixes n' fucks
inna burned out crack
house
near Chalmers n'
Jefferson
tryin'
to git this here 26 gauge
needle
this rusty needle
inta the vein
in my groin
you know
into that little hole
i've used so many time
before
you know
the black one
oozing pus n'black
blood
that little hole
I've hit so many times
before
You know
you know
the one with the ugly
rash
and infection around it
you know the one

and 'm tryin' at feel
good again
like, you know
like I did
so long before
me hands
me poor hands
me sad ol' hands
is all black n' blue
and swollen
me swollen hands
swollen like boxing
gloves
and so swollen you know
that my crusty fingers
my ugly little fingers
don't work properly
you know
and I'm foolin'
me the fool
me the fool
I'm foolin'
with this used rig
I found on the floor
me the fool
me the junky fool
me
the shit goin' solid in the
syringe
and I can't even git a fucking hit
i can't
but it's gonna be alright
you know
cuz I'm gonna git it
together
you know
I'm gonna git it

together
you know
real soon
I am
man I ain't shit in 2
weeks from that fucken
methadone
and I got this case comin' up
for dealin'
but my friends in line at
the clinic
bin tellin' me how to
survive in prison
and I got busted agin
last week
with a bundle with a
bundle
but it ain't about nothin'
cuz I got a good mouth-
piece
right?
But my veins are all
gone
my blood black veins
all gone
except for what's left of
this one
in my groin
But it ain't working
and I'm bogue as shit
and my lover O.D.'d last week
man
I woke up from a 14
year nod
and she was just a lyin' there
on her back
on her back man

nude, man
there she was nude
onner back
dead stiff n' cold
with this mouth
this gaping mouth
man
this wide open mouth
teeth barred like some
sick demon fangs
with evil foam all over
her face
and man she just turned 23
and I loved her as they
took her out inna black plastic
body bag
(she hated plastic
you know)
But I'm tryin' to get off
crap
as I think about how I ripped off
my parents silverware
for this fix
dig
and I'm broke
but it's alright cuz
I'm gonna get it together
next week
ok?
My feet are so swollen
that I can't tie up
me shoes
and I piss blood
and I can't eat without
pukin'
so I'm livin on
McDonalds milkshakes

but
I know
there's sumptin' bad wrong with my stomach
and my hairs fallin' out
in clumps
my skin is green
and
I need to see a dentist
cuz my teeth are rottin'
but it's cool
cuz I'ma gonna get this hit
this here hit
this one hit
and bang these 4 paks
even tho it ain't working
and I'm tired
I'm sick and tired
I am
tired
so sick n' tired
I'm so fucking sick and tired
and lonely
and alone
and I keep goin' under cuz I'm shootin so much
dig
even tho the shit aint getting me off
but I tell you what man
I'll tell you what
I say I'll tell you what
man I'm gonna get it together soon man
I really am
I am
I really am
dig
and it's all cool anyway
cuz heroin is so fucking hip

Finding Forrest's writings increased my awareness of what he was going through. He'd hidden his deepest despairs from me when he was alive.

When Forrest first joined AA, the organization frowned upon the medications he was taking to control bipolar disease, so he discontinued them. He became delusional and was on the streets for about three weeks. He would call and tell us where he was, and we would rush over there, but he'd be gone.

I worried constantly. Where was he, and what was happening to him? I didn't know how he was eating and where he was sleeping. He got off drugs, which was a great accomplishment, but now the bipolar disease had grabbed him again. I waited for the phone to ring, and then when it would, I'd panic.

After about three weeks, I got a phone call from Forrest telling me, "Mom, I'm on my way to Florida, but I can't tell you exactly where I am because the FBI is after me. Please help me."

I told him, "Of course, I will, but I have to know where you are in order to help. Please tell me where you are." He immediately hung up the phone. I heard from him sporadically over the next couple weeks. I never knew where he was and how he was getting by. The worry hung over me like a cloud. I could never shake it.

I finally got a call from a hospital in Key West. The nurse said, "Forrest is in the mental part of our hospital. He will not eat or take medication because he believes that someone is trying to poison him. He originally went to the hospital because he was so weak from not eating. He was sure all the food was poisoned. Will you come to a hearing to have Forrest committed?"

I was so grateful to hear that he was in a safe place that I immediately said, "Yes, when will that be?"

"Tomorrow," she told me.

So Gerry and I drove to Key West and went to the courthouse. While standing in the hallway, Forrest was brought in in handcuffs. He wouldn't look or talk to me. He was convinced that I was his enemy. I was devastated; it was a very low point in my life.

We all sat down, and Forrest pled with the hospital staff to release him. If no one knew better, they'd think he was completely rational. He turned to me and said, "Mom, why won't you help me?"

I answered, "Forrest, I am." He turned his head and didn't look at me again. I realized it was the disease talking and not Forrest. Knowing that, it was still hard to see my beloved son think he was well when he wasn't. Thankfully, Forrest was denied his request. He was committed and taken back to the hospital.

A week later we got a call from Forrest. He was himself again. The medication was working. Gerry and I drove to Key West again, took him out to lunch, bought him some clothes, and had a wonderful visit. After his release, he visited us for a short time and then eventually went back to Michigan. That crisis was over.

* * *

Forrest had been on a path of destruction for years. He helped himself by getting off drugs, going to Narcotics Anonymous (NA) and AA meetings, and counseling young people. He was doing so well, and then disaster struck. His bipolar illness got out of control, and he couldn't handle living on this planet; his depression was just too severe. It overpowered him and caused him to do whatever was necessary for him to put out the fire. He couldn't stay here; it was too hot. I hate fires of any kind, but most of all that one.

* * *

CHAPTER 5

STARTING TO HEAL

I got a copy of a book written by Forrest's psychiatrist, Jaswant Bagga, M.D., called, "Living with Dignity." He told me he'd written something about Forrest in the chapter called, 'Human Suffering. "'This particular piece was written under the subhead, 'People Help People All the Time, But Sometimes, They Don't Even Know It:'

> One day about 10 in the morning a man came to see me. He was extremely intelligent and he had thoroughly studied all the medications he had ever taken. I don't recall how, but we began talking about Reglan (Metoclopramide), a medication that he had used for stomach trouble. He told me so much more about it than I had ever known before. As soon as he left, I quickly looked up

> Reglan in the physician desk reference, and all the information he gave to me, had been correct.
>
> Now this is the amazing part. The same day, in the afternoon, a lady came in and among a few other complaints, she described that she was very sad about the fact that her family doctor suspected a Pituitary tumor in her brain and that he had scheduled her for a number of tests including the most expensive one, MRI. The reason for this suspicion of tumor was that she had experienced abnormal secretion of milk from her breast and a prolactin level was quite high.
>
> I asked her what medication she was taking and interestingly, she said, "just this Reglan." My eyes opened up and expanded 10 times their normal size. My measly little brain had figured out a real problem. A few hours ago, my intellectual patient had told me clearly that many phenothiazine drugs, Reglan could cause milk secretion and a high prolactin level.
>
> My brilliant patient helped her a great deal and didn't even know he was helping. She was amazed at my knowledge. I silently thanked God for helping me. She stopped the Reglan and sure enough, within a few days, her symptoms vanished and prolactin level fell to normal.

It helped me to go over Forrest's life. I told Gerry, "I need to do something to help me heal, to get out of the hole of sadness I'm in. I want to go on a different path." I got an idea on Forrest's birthday, the second one after he left and decided that I'd stop drinking in his honor. He'd been in the AA program for five years, but I'd never gone to

Al-anon. I'd continued to drink wine when he was around, never thinking what a difficult task it was for him every day of his life not to take a drug or drink.

I don't know what I was thinking at that time, but I'm not proud of it. Forrest had done such a remarkable job of getting off drugs, and I wanted him to know how proud I was of him. I believed that he'd know that on the other side. It was a small step, and I took it. I haven't taken a drink since that day. I went to meetings, which helped me, and greatly admired the people who chose the path of AA. I got an insight into what Forrest had experienced at his meetings, and it made me feel closer to him.

Not drinking helped, but I was still living a nightmare and wanted to wake up from it. No more Forrest—I still couldn't believe it! I wanted to run away and leave my problems behind. Maybe I could find someplace where my emotions and thinking could be rearranged. That wouldn't be hard to find, would it? I knew I had to incorporate something new into my daily routine to ensure that I wouldn't drink.

When Forrest was in high school he'd asked me, "Mom, will you do Transcendental Meditation with me?" I never did. All I can say is that I'm looking through my present eyes, which have more wisdom and knowledge, not my past ones.

It seemed like the perfect time to start meditating, so I set out to find how to accomplish that. I contacted an assistant of Dr. Deepak Chopra's and she said, "There's a teaching seminar next week in Ann Arbor, Michigan. You'll learn the fundamentals of meditating."

I eagerly attended and got my primordial sound, which is the sound of the earth when one is born. Dr. Chopra is able to put the date, time, and location when one is born into a computer and figure out what the sound of the earth was at that time. The sound resonates with me now because it's familiar to me.

I started meditating twice daily, a half-hour in the morning immediately after rising, and a half-hour in the afternoon. I created an altar, which has special objects on it that mean a great deal to me: stones from Gerry, an angel Valarie gave to me, a little jade Buddha from Forrest, a note from my stepsons, a St. Patrick's Day shamrock from a close friend, a special crystal from another friend, and other crystals. These are nice reminders that I'm surrounded with love. I suppose I could look at it as my island of love.

Some days, a beautiful bluebird perched on a tree is singing a melody that filled my ears with joy. He was awake, happy, and greeted the day with his song. I started greeting every day with meditation. It was and is important for me to have this ritual. The bluebird sings, and I sing in my own way. I'm not perched on a branch of a tree, but I meditate in my favorite chair in front of my altar.

Thoughts came in and went out at that time, some disturbing and some uplifting. The problem was, I didn't seem to be able to control the process. I was unable to pick and choose, but I did find help in meditation. It was food for my soul—a safe, familiar harbor for me. I was dining on the elixir of my being. I slowed down my thoughts, and it didn't even cost any money. Meditation quieted my mind as I sat in front of my altar and used my primordial sound for 30 minutes. My body, mind, and soul took to it and relished being there. What could be better? My body relaxed, and my mind started clearing.

Meditation was like going to a well every day, dropping a bucket down, pulling it up and getting delicious water to drink. I needed to nourish my body with water in order to function and I needed to nourish my soul with meditation in order to flourish. I went into a space that was very peaceful and sometimes I got answers to problems I was trying to work out. They just came to me.

I've talked to other people who meditate, and they say the exact same thing. If their day is stressed, they stop to meditate in the middle of the day and immediately slow down and regain focus. Meditation truly helped me to heal.

Another healing modality I used was yoga. My body actually shook at times during the long months after

Forrest left. It reacted to the storm that ravaged my life. At times, I appeared to have a calmness embedded in me, but that was deceiving. The storm would abate, and then it would surface again out of nowhere. I knew I had to do more.

I also found out that stress has power. When stress arrives, it steers the ship. No one else can get to the helm because stress has taken over. The question for me was: how could I remove stress from the helm? Then, along came yoga. It taught me how to breathe correctly and relieve stress.

There are two kinds of breathing that I learned to do.

1. Deep breathing . . . breathe through the nose, starting from the stomach and out through the nose . . . continue to the count of ten.
2. Alternate nose breathing . . . it has been practiced for centuries. It helps purify the body and calm the mind and has been known to have a balancing effect for the right and left hemispheres of the brain.

    a. Use your right thumb to cover your right nostril. Keep your right nostril closed with your right thumb while breathing in for four counts through your left nostril.
    b. Close off your left nostril with your middle finger . . . hold both nostrils closed for eight counts.
    c. At the end of eight counts, release you thumb from your right nostril and exhale out of that side for another four counts.
    d. Inhale through your right nostril for four counts and close both nostrils. Hold for eight counts and release the your middle finger from your left nostril while exhaling for four counts.
    e. Inhale through your left nostril for four counts and close both nostrils. Hold for eight counts and release the thumb from your right nostril while exhaling for four counts. Repeat the full cycle ten times.

Around this time, a meteorite blasted out of the sky and landed in an uninhabited area. People from all over ran to observe what had happened. It certainly got their attention. I thought that maybe a meteorite would come down and give me instructions on what else I could do. Answers can arrive in different ways. One was the Mental Illness Research Association (MIRA), a nonprofit organization that funds research and education projects.

One Thursday evening in September 1995, Forrest's father called and said, "I saw an article in the paper that mentioned a mental health organization called MIRA. They're going to have a gala dinner tomorrow night. I called the president and asked him if I could get tickets. It was sold out, but he was able to find a couple. Would you like to buy them?"

Gerry turned from the phone and said to me, "Let's go. I think it would be good to get involved with an organization like that." I agreed.

The following night we dressed in our evening clothes and went to the dinner. We didn't know anyone, but everyone was friendly and greeted us warmly. The tables were beautiful, and music was softly playing in the background. The energy was exhilarating.

We were seated at a table with doctors who were involved with mental health. We later found out that most of the people who attended had a connection with a loved one, relative, or friend suffering from a mental disease. After dinner, we listened to a heartfelt talk given by the president's son, Patrick, who also had a mental disease. He talked about his struggles, how hard it was to make it, and how he sometimes almost didn't. We were moved by this young man and couldn't help but identify with Forrest. It took such courage for him to tell his story. I found comfort and felt like we belonged there.

Then there was a raffle, and we had purchased a ticket. Dick Puritan, a well-known radio personality in Michigan, was the emcee. He came onto the stage and announced that the drawing was about to start. There was both a $5,000 and a $10,000 prize. He drew the ticket for the first prize, but we didn't win. After that announcement, Gerry said, "If we win the $10,000, we will donate it to the organization, won't we?"

"Yes, definitely," I answered. We held our breath while the name of the winner for the last prize was drawn. Dick Puritan pulled out the ticket and said our names. We were stunned. We won! We got out of our chairs and briskly walked onto the stage. Dick congratulated us, and we immediately said, "We're going to donate this prize to MIRA." Everyone cheered, and we did, too. A feeling came over me that all of this was meant to be. It was the universe at work.

Patrick, the founder and president, asked us if we'd like to become members of MIRA, and we readily agreed. That was the beginning of a worthwhile time for us and helped me along my healing path. We became board members, and supported a MIRA research project called "The Arthur Forrest Tull, II Memorial Fund," sponsored by the University of Michigan. There are 185,000 suicides per year worldwide. Parents don't imagine that their children will leave the planet before they do, much less that the end of their children's lives can come about so violently.

Gerry designed and implemented a mental-health education awareness program that has been introduced to over 800 schools in the state of Michigan. This program was designed to bring teachers and students up-to-date about the latest findings in brain science and to remove the stigma associated with mental diseases. Our dream is that all of these brain diseases and disorders will be viewed in the same light as any other disease. It will take time, but it can be accomplished.

We joined MIRA because we felt that if we could save one family or child from going through what we experienced, it was worth it. I know we did help other families, I just don't know how many. I was president for three years, and Forrest was my guiding light. Helping others verified his life and his leaving. MIRA carries on its work, which we still support.

* * *

CHAPTER 6

RENATA

I was still struggling with the loss of Forrest, although my life was returning to a semblance of normalcy. However, a dark cloud was still hanging over me. I continued to miss my son but was having fewer moments of despair. Everything I was doing helped immensely—abstaining from alcohol, meditation, yoga, and my day-to-day involvement with MIRA. I was moving along my path of healing but had a long way to go. My daughter, Valarie, helped me find the ultimate healer.

Valarie was born two-and-a-half years after Forrest. She was a happy child and inquisitive about everything as she grew up. She had an innate wisdom that particularly related to other people. But when she was in high school, bipolar disorder struck. She was misdiagnosed and put on the wrong medication, just like her brother, and consequently had some difficult times. She fought this formidable foe and has been doing so ever since. She's been knocked down more than a few times, but she always gets up and starts anew. Bipolar disease has not won, and I don't think it ever will. It makes life challenging for her, but she manages to overcome it.

Back in 1999, Valarie was in a difficult period of her life, dealing with deep depression. The doctors changed her medication, and she was undergoing therapy, but nothing helped. Two of my friends, Phyllis and Beverly, said, "We went to a woman named Renata Moore, an intuitive counselor, who was highly recommended to us. She's remarkable. We both talked to our loved ones on the other side, and she helped us resolve many issues. Maybe Valarie would benefit from seeing her." I agreed to contact her.

I made an appointment for Valarie, and we met Renata at her office. When she stood to greet us, I immediately thought, She seems like a kind individual. There's an aura of warmth and compassion surrounding her. She exuded quiet competence, which I could almost palpably feel.

After talking to Valarie for a length of time, Renata said that she felt she could help her. She told us, "I'll fit Valarie into my schedule in the evenings to begin with. It's important for me to see her immediately on an intensive basis."

Renata worked with Valarie and helped her immensely. She was able to guide her through her many issues and lift her out of her depression. Renata told me, "Valarie is the highest-functioning bipolar I've ever counseled. I lived with and counseled bipolar women while I was getting my master's degree. She will grow like a sunflower with her face lifted to the sun."

Placing that phone call was one of the most significant actions I've ever taken. I was frightened because Valarie was so depressed, I thought about Forrest all the time and what had happened to him. If it happened to one of my children, I worried that it could happen to both. I tried to maintain an even keel, but I was having great difficulty along the way. I began seeing Renata individually to discuss my role in helping Valarie come out of her depression. After a while, it was quite apparent that I could use Renata's help, also. That started a ten-year extraordinary relationship where I went into territory I'd never explored before.

During one of our first sessions, Renata explained, "We all have a shadow. In that shadow are all of the unresolved issues that we have tucked away." She took a box from a drawer in her desk, opened the lid, and said, "What is in there is the shadow. It remains hidden until we decide we can take it out, usually in increments. After each piece of the shadow is brought forth, examined and accepted in the light, there's a shift of consciousness." She paused and continued, "When a shift in consciousness happens, one looks at all situations from a different perspective." I didn't realize at that time how painful that could be.

Renata helped me deal with and understand old problems from childhood. I'd always had a turbulent relationship with my mother, and I suspected that there were lots of shadows relating to her in that box. There were. I had a loving relationship with my father, but the one with my mother was entirely different. It appeared that she didn't like me or love me, and I couldn't understand why.

For example, she made disparaging remarks about my physical appearance. I thought at that time, Maybe it would be different if I were pretty. If I had a different color hair or was a boy, then she would like me. After all, she likes and loves my brothers—that must be the answer. BE A BOY!

I remember vividly when I was four years old that I would kneel by the side of the bed every night, put my hands together, and pray, "Dear God, please, take me back to heaven and make me a boy." I would wake up in the morning and be devastated because it hadn't happened. Unfortunately, I was still a girl.

My parents had to take me to the doctor when I was nine years old because I hardly ate and was stick thin. The doctor gave me a horrible-tasting thick medicine to drink every day. It didn't help. Perhaps love from my mother would have nourished me, but that wasn't possible.

Renata had the ability to see energy fields around the body and could determine what was bothering me. After months of seeing her and knowing what was on my mind, I asked, "How are you able to know what's bothering me?"

She told me, "I see emotions that you're experiencing at the moment in your aura." She could pick out what was challenging for me even if I wasn't aware. I couldn't hide anything if I wanted to. She was the voice of sanity and reason and knew me like no one else did. She accepted and loved me completely. What a rare gift to have in life.

My relationship with my father came up during the discussions of my mother. My dad was my beacon, my mast in the storm and my link to happiness. I knew I couldn't rely on him completely because his loyalty was first to my mother, but most of the time I felt safe with him. I knew how much he loved me. He would say, "Mary Jean, your mother is sick." I couldn't see any evidence of physical disease, but now I know that it was a mental illness. It was implied that I was the one responsible for making the relationship work. I was supposed to be the adult. The problem was, no matter what I did, it didn't seem to make any difference.

I remember as a small child, lying on my back on the soft green grass in our front yard and looking up at the white puffy clouds in the sky. I would dream of a different life. "I'll be a princess and be adored by many, and then I will be loved." Or, "I'll be a movie star like Shirley Temple—she sings, dances, and says perfect words—then I will be loved." Or, "I'll change how I look, maybe have blonde hair instead of dark brown—then I will be loved."

My mother didn't like the way I looked or acted, so it made sense to me that if I were someone else, then she would treat me differently. The daydreaming always related to the reality that I didn't feel loved. The hurt cut a deep gash into my soul, and I didn't think it would ever heal. I would always hope that I'd come out of my daydreams and be loved by my mother. But that dream was never fulfilled. However, working with Renata healed that relationship. It took many sessions of opening the box, putting a little back in, and then pulling more out. That was a huge step toward my recovery.

I would be in a session with Renata and all of a sudden she would take deep yawns. I wondered why she did that at a certain point but never asked her about it, until one day my curiosity got the better of me. I asked, "What happens when you yawn?"

She said, "Your dad and Forrest have been coming in. My energy changes when they do so. I've been giving you the advice they offer."

I was thrilled but skeptical. She hadn't told me what was happening because she knew it would be a lot for me to absorb, and also knew I would doubt on a very deep level that she was talking to them. She was right. Looking back, I don't quite understand why I felt that way because where else would she be getting the information? She told me things no one would know but them. All I can say is that that was my mind-set at the time. I'd gone to psychics in the past, but I didn't think they talked to the spirits. I thought they had powers to pick up messages from the universe and had the ability to see into the future. That was the beginning of some of the most interesting days of my life, and a huge part of my healing.

My father primarily came in the first couple of years to help me with my childhood issues. Forrest came with him most of the time, but Dad would do most of the talking. He'd come in and say, "Hi, honey, I miss you. I'd like an afternoon of talk. I'm communicating through the airwaves. I love you a lot and respect you. Forrest and I get together and talk about you and how much we miss you."

He told me, "In retrospect, I can see how difficult your mother made your life. I am deeply sorry and regret what happened. I didn't know all that was going on, especially when I wasn't home. I knew she treated you differently than your brothers, but I didn't realize the extent of the emotional abuse."

I told him, "I'm angry with you for not stepping in and protecting me when I was little."

He responded, "I understand how you feel. I want to help you work out your relationship with your mother for your own health. If you continue to carry around the sorrow and anger, it will affect your health. You insist on judging your mother in the past. You're hampered by the past. Mother has a hold on you because you can't let go. Move on in life . . . into the now."

He continued, "You are breaking through old barriers. There's an old feeling from when you were little that something happened that wasn't right. You're gaining wisdom and knowledge. Your diligence to change what doesn't work is why you're here today. You are working toward happiness and peace." Renata told me that Dad would show her a huge bouquet of flowers and describe how beautiful they were. He loved flowers as much as I do.

I could be completely exhausted when I was on my way to see Renata and then walk out of her office energized. Renata said, "Forrest and Dad send you energy." I was amazed by the amount I would receive. It happened to me every time they came in to help me. Renata told me, "I receive great energy, also."

I was quite busy at that time. I was president of MIRA and also president of our Association in Florida. I was constantly on the go, convinced that I had to stay busy all the time so I wouldn't look at what was hidden deep in my psyche.

One time Dad said through Renata, "It's good to rest on planet Earth. The idea is that we have to be doing something all the time. You're nervous and high strung because of the confusion in our home while growing up. You stayed busy to keep away from Mother. You miss the essence of life when you stay extremely busy. You can feel safe now. I have a sincere regret that I didn't keep you safe."

I went to Renata's one day, particularly sad about Forrest leaving and feeling that I was responsible, still hanging on to the idea that I could have stopped him. Dad came in immediately after the session started.

He said, "You couldn't have stopped Forrest even if you had been in the next room."

I was stunned that he knew what I'd been dealing with that day. But I shouldn't have been. Those words were very consoling to me and started to change my thinking.

He also told me, "I'm so happy to have a medium to come through. There are many souls here who would like a connection with their loved ones on the planet. I often walk with you because I didn't do that enough when I was there. Energy from nature is restorative." His love constantly flowed to me.

One day, Dad came in and surprised me by bringing one of my favorite aunts, Aunt Jane, with him. She'd left the planet about a year earlier after a long life. She'd had 13 children, and one had died shortly after birth. She and my uncle John lived on a large farm in Ohio, and she'd worked hard throughout her life. She was physically lovely, spiritually bright, very interesting, and a great mother. We became quite close toward the end of her life, and I considered our relationship a real privilege. I still miss talking to her on the phone.

She said, "Mary Jean, now I know the key to happiness on the planet is to be in a balanced state all of the time. You can blink your eyes and you can see things differently. I am so happy to be here. It's magnificent. It's most enjoyable coming back home. I'm thrilled to connect with you. You're a pioneer, and there's a master plan. Would we be working with you so closely if you didn't have the same qualities we have? Forrest is around you a lot. He's very connected, and what he's doing is quite impressive." Renata told me many times that Forrest was very evolved in the spiritual world. I was to find out more as time went along.

When Aunt Jane talked about balance, it resonated with me. I realized I needed that in my life. But how would I get it? I knew I could balance my body by what I fed it, but how could I feed my mind to achieve balance?

I would be looking out the window at beautiful huge white snowflakes falling down from the sky, creating a dense white blanket on the ground. The trees would be covered as though they'd been dressed to have their picture taken. It seemed pristine and new. I remember thinking, If only life could always be like this—with peace, quiet, and beauty. My life had these moments of tranquility, and I relished them but needed more. But how?

I had to find the key to the door of happiness. I couldn't have excess in my life. I had to find the strength to do that.

"Balance! I must be balanced." I realized that that was the main ingredient. I didn't have to change the outer world to experience balance. It was all within me—first the awareness, then determining how to go about achieving it. I had to change my perspective—clear out the old and make room for the new. I couldn't continue to embrace my old ways of thinking. Meditation, yoga, and Renata could help me make the shift.

* * *

CHAPTER 7

CONVERSATIONS WITH FORREST

As time went on, Forrest started coming in more often. I couldn't see him or touch him, but I could talk to him through Renata. I found a connection, and my world changed. At first, I had my doubts; contacting someone from the other side was hard for me to grasp. I was a doubting Thomas, thinking that seeing was believing.

Forrest knew that I had my doubts, and he'd make a point of saying something so I would know this was all true. One morning while I was brushing my teeth, I picked up the little paper cup that I use for water and noticed that there were sweet little bluebirds drawn on it. I thought, I love bluebirds. I had used these cups for a long time and had never taken notice before.

I went to see Renata that day, and after she'd made contact with Forrest, she asked me, "Do bluebirds mean anything to you?"

I'd forgotten about the morning incident, so I said no. Renata asked, "Are you sure?" and I told her I was positive. She then said, "Forrest said, 'Mother, I love bluebirds, too.'" I immediately remembered and was elated.

Renata told me, "Forrest is telling you that so that you know these conversations are real." My skepticism lifted, and my heart soared upon hearing this confirmation. This was the first time I truly started to believe that all of the communications were true. It's true that seeing is believing, but I realized I didn't actually have to see to believe.

One of the first things Forrest said to me was: "Life is good. Live every day. I am okay. Look to the sky and you will see me."

I said, "I don't understand."

Forrest replied, "I come in just under the clouds. I'm not in my ashes—there's no energy there. Keep them to console yourself. I love you. We are never more than one thought away. I miss you deeply."

The tears started falling out of my eyes and rolled down my face. I couldn't seem to stop the avalanche of water. It was if the tears had been stored up for years and were finally breaking forth. I was surprised by how they seemed to have an urgency about them. We must get out, we must get out, seemed to be the message. They were tears of joy. I was connecting with my son and having a relationship; it just happened to be on another level. I couldn't see him, but he could see me.

Over a span of ten years, Forrest and I had many conversations. I began to understand him like I never had before. He told me many times how sad he was because of the pain he'd inflicted on all of us by leaving. In fact, one day tears even poured from Renata's eyes. She said, "Forrest is crying on the other side, and I always cry when the spirit cries. He never meant to hurt Valarie and you, but he knew it was time to go."

Forrest said:

> "The spirit called me home. My spirit said, 'You have a chance to go home now.' There was nothing personal against you, Mom. There is nothing you could have done to change the outcome. I pretended to have my reality in control. It was hard to manipulate my reality, and when I couldn't, I left. The last two years of my life, I was not myself. I blamed other people, and I couldn't find a way out. I gave up hope. Mom, you are not responsible.
>
> "Mom, you were consistent for me. When there is no consistency, one doesn't know what happens from one day to another. Part of what you provided for me, in a very deep way, was safety. You gave me freedom of life, Mom. Please, don't remember me by my suicide. I'm sorry for the way I left, but I finally have freedom. You can never really know freedom until you're here. There were lots of wonderful times. I am sorry there was no closure. Please don't be sad. I'm free. We're all coming here. I lost my way. I've learned so much here and remembered I was not balanced. I have not left you. I have gone from physical son to spiritual son. We all have our awakening. I had to earn back your trust. I deceived you. I take responsibility for my actions."

Forrest lied to me many times while he was taking drugs. It reached the point where I felt that I could never believe him, and I didn't for a long time.

He also said, "Mom, I'm grateful that the three of us have found a way of communicating because nothing is better than talking to you, nothing better. We are here for you."

I answered, "Forrest, that is so wonderful. I feel the same way. Talking with you has made it so that I'm not in the depths I was when you left this planet. I understand how happy you are, and that makes me happy. I feel the love that you are transmitting to me. I feel it all the time; it's bountiful."

Forrest said, "Mother I am so much more effective over here. I feel much better being effective and not being swamped with my own feelings and emotions."

I felt like I was in a cocoon of love when I talked to him on the other side. He was extremely happy, so much so that I could never wish him back.

Forrest also told me, "Mom, death is not final. I stepped out of my body. My spiritual, immortal side left. I've gone to critical mass. Between womb and birth, we forget all experiences from other lives and the other side. I've learned lessons. One day we will be together."

I thought about that and remembered when I was in eighth grade getting ready for the big day of my graduation. I thought it was one of the most important days of my life. The day before my graduation, we received a phone call telling us, "Dad passed away from a cerebral hemorrhage today." He was my mother's father, only 68 years old. I was devastated because I loved my grandfather very much, and selfishly, I knew I'd have to miss graduation.

I was a little afraid of my grandfather; he was a looming figure to me. He talked with a Boston accent, never smoked or drank, and loved to play cards. One of my fondest memories is seeing him sitting on the front-porch swing of my grandparents' home while my cousins and I were waiting to see who would be the chosen one to comb his hair that day. He was practically bald, so the gesture was simply symbolic, but it was his way of finding a reason to give us a nickel. I would wait for him to give me the honor by saying, "Mary Jean, comb my hair today." I would eagerly and with gratitude pick up his comb that had narrow teeth on one side and full teeth on the other half, and comb his hair with great care for a few minutes. That made me feel special for the entire day.

He was laid to rest in my grandparents' home, but I wasn't fond of being around his body in the casket. My aunts and my mother wanted me to kiss him as he lay in the casket and said, "Kiss him, Mary Jean, kiss him. Grandpa loved you very much." I finally did. I hated it; it scared me half to death. What a gruesome thing to make a child do. But that was the custom in my mother's family. I was incredibly upset afterward and knew I would never do that again.

That was my first exposure to someone leaving this planet. It was all so mysterious. Did my grandfather die in sin or in a state of grace? He was in another woman's home when he passed away, so I concluded that he was in a state of sin. I was fearful for him and afraid of death.

The pivotal moment of awareness that I had with respect to what really happens when we exit from this planet was when my late husband passed away. Valarie and I had been at his bedside for a day and a half. He was in a coma after a long battle with cancer. After taking his last breath, we saw a light beneath his skin that then spiraled up and out of the top of his head and left. We looked at each other in disbelief and said, "Did you see that? That's beautiful." That was an important piece of my quest to find answers.

This feeling was magnified when Forrest left. I knew in the depths of my soul that he had also gone someplace else. He simply shrugged off his body and left. There was great consolation in knowing that. I continue to have a relationship with Forrest, spiritually rather than physically.

Today I accept death as a natural occurrence. There's nothing to fear. I believe I will fly off, reunite with my loved ones, and continue my journey over there.

> Forrest continued:
>
> "I'm so very pleased and amazed at what I'm getting done here. I'm happy to be in spirit; it gets better. I'm overwhelmed with

emotion. Being your son is a big part of my evolution. I'm recognizing patterns that kept me from my own spirit. I didn't communicate about my life and how I felt. I lost the battle of Forrest.

"I am a teacher in mystery schools. I have been given tools, not like the schools on the planet. I realize the difference between reality and illusion. Nothing appears as it is; it is all illusion on the planet. I'm teaching how to separate illusion from reality. Illusion keeps you trapped in a world of judgment. Life is too short to get caught up in the material world. It's not what you have; it's what you are that's important. Be aware of choices."

I know that I do make choices, but I didn't understand how all-encompassing those choices were predicated on past experiences. It took me a long time to do that. I was able to by bringing forth the shadow with Renata's help.

Forrest also knew I was doing yoga and meditating.

He said:

"Yoga opens up space in the body to hold more of the spiritual body. Keep it balanced. Meditation keeps balance—not fantasy, just reality. It is time for you to put your emotional energy into neutral. Put your inner critic on neutral. Don't judge your emotions. Be gentle on yourself. Awareness can come in when you are in neutral, and then you can observe and not judge. Being caught in the trap of judgment makes life difficult."

FORREST GAVE ME STEPS ON HOW TO ATTAIN HAPPINESS AND LIVE HARMONIOUSLY

ATTAINMENT OF TRUE HAPPINESS

1. Peace with oneself and the world
2. To be content with the past
3. Thankful for the present
4. Patience for the future and expectant toward all that it promise

TO LIVE THIS IS TO LIVE HARMONIOUSLY

SECRET OF HARMONY

1. Be willing to have an uncluttered mind
2. Be willing to be taught
3. Be willing to forgive

* * *

CHAPTER 8

INSIGHTS AND MEMORIES

After seeing Renata for about a year and a half, she recommended that I receive a healing technique called "Barbara Brennan's Hand of Healing." I was familiar with Brennan because I'd read her book. I looked forward all week to the session, and the day finally arrived. I went to Renata's office and laid down on a massage table. A young man who had trained under Barbara started putting his hands on and over me. Renata took notes and, at times, guided him.

I became very emotional and started to cry. But that was the point: to bring up old emotions that needed to be healed. I could tell that it benefited me because I felt relieved when it was over. I sat up and looked at Renata and saw a white round spirit with beautiful laughing eyes there instead of her. I looked over at the other therapist, saw him clearly, looked back at Renata, and still saw her spirit. It was a beautiful sight to behold. I'd never seen anything like that, and I was in awe.

As soon as we were alone, I told Renata about my experience and asked her, "Has any other client experienced that?"

She said, "No, some clients have seen the people with whom I communicate on the other side, but you're the only one who has ever seen my spirit." I was thrilled to be so privileged. It was another confirmation to me that we can see things that aren't part of this dimension.

I was in my yoga class one day, and we were working on our chakras. I had my eyes closed, and when I opened them, I saw that everyone had a green face from their mouth up. Not believing what I was seeing, I quickly closed my eyes, opened them again, and still saw the same sight. There were no mirrors in the room, so I couldn't see my own face. I didn't know what was happening, and it frightened me. I just stood and stared at everyone. What was going on? Was there something wrong with my eyes? I was stunned. The episode lasted about ten minutes and left as fast as it came.

I told Renata about it, and she told me, "You saw chakra colors. Each color represents a chakra." I was no longer frightened. I'd heard of chakras but didn't know they had colors.

The next time in class, I saw white on the face of Carol, the yoga teacher, and then the most beautiful color blue completely covered her face. It seemed to hang there. I approached her with apprehension and said, "I'm seeing chakra colors of white, green, and blue around you."

She put her hands together and said, "Praise the Lord." Since then I've seen red around her, the color of the root chakra. It spirals up to the ceiling and down behind to the floor. I told her, and she said, "I've been working on my root chakra, which is red."

Some days I saw many colors and would say, "Today was a very colorful day." She liked that. I only saw the colors during Carol's yoga class.

My heart swells when I see chakra colors. Their brilliance is hard to capture in paint. The white is the purest chalk-white I've ever seen. The blue is heavenly, and the red has an intensity that I've never seen before. Yellow is bright, yet warm. My eyes could look at these colors forever. There's a splendor about them. I can't go to a paint store to buy them, and I can't foretell when they will appear; they just do.

Colors have always brightened my life. I love the colors of a rainbow, the perfect arc up into the sky with colors not made by man, just there to marvel at and enjoy. As a child, I was told about the gold at the end of the rainbow, and always looked for it but never found it. I think that seeing the rainbow is tantamount to finding the gold—there's a beauty that can't be touched, but is available for all to see and enjoy.

* * *

After writing about all that beauty, there's something that I'm reluctant to write about, but it's part of my life experience so I feel I should. I was sexually abused as a child. My parents were never aware of it, and even I didn't recall it for years.

When I first let it out of the shadow, I completely rejected the whole idea. I thought I was making it up. Renata and I kept working on it until finally all of the memories and feelings were out in the open. I will admit that it was a tough process and hard to get there. The threat of thinking it was my fault was always there, and I couldn't face it. I know who did it. I'd never liked him as I was growing up, and he was someone I was afraid of, and I didn't understand my feelings. He lived with us for a while, and that's when it happened. It was a disgusting occurrence. He took a sexual act for adults and degraded me as a child for his own sick pleasure. There's no other way to say it.

Renata explained why it was so hard to even look at the abuse. "When children are sexually abused, they dissociate and go into a part of the mind because of the pain happening at the moment. The body has a response to stimuli known as pleasure that they can't control. The child feels shame; the body feels pleasure. The memory is in the unconscious."

When he found out about the abuse, my dad told me, "Your mother and I didn't know what happened. If we had, there would have been severe repercussions for that man. Let the past go back to the past. Clear the past and allow yourself to live in the present time."

Renata told me, "Before you can get rid of all of the sickening invasions done to you, you most forgive. Forgiveness is not condoning what was done, but it frees you."

I knew she was right, but forgiving was difficult after being hurt. The pain seared deeply within me. It was hard for me to open my heart and let the hurt leave my body. It seemed stuck there, painful but content to remain. How could I release it? Why was it stuck to me? I could visualize it being a piece of sheer plastic that I could grab, and it would stick to my hand. I would transfer it to the other, and it would still be there. It just didn't want to leave.

I wondered what I could do. I considered that I could allow my heart to give out love, but my body and mind immediately fought this request from my heart. I kept telling myself that forgiving doesn't mean condoning the actions that resulted in hurt. Forgiving heals. I didn't even have to carry the scars. They would fade in time. My heart could send out beams of love to heal me. I knew I could forgive the person because he created it, and I didn't have to accept his creation anymore. I wanted to create anew. I wanted to heal my psyche and allow new memories to take the place of the hurt.

I am free now because I've forgiven this man. I will never condone his actions, but I don't want to get sick emotionally and physically by holding unforgiving feelings inside me. He must atone at some point. He's been out of my life for a long time, so I'm sure he had to do that where he is. A wave of water washes over me and cleanses all parts of me. I am free.

* * *

Not all of my memories from childhood are grim. There were certainly delightful ones. One time, Mom, dad, my brothers, and I piled into the car to visit our grandparents in Ohio for an exciting adventure. My father stood in front of the car and cranked the engine. Dad jumped back into the car and said, "Off we go." We ate sandwiches and fruit from a picnic basket along the way. There weren't many restaurants along the highway (before expressways) and few gas stations. We went down the highway singing songs, counting the clouds in the sky, and figuring out what they looked like.

It took us many hours to get to the house because we had to travel on two-lane roads. My stomach churned with excitement as we neared Grandma and Grandpa's house. The impending joy was hardly containable. We reached the small town, went over a bridge, and saw all the familiar sights. We were getting close now! Finally, we arrived. I raced out of the car into the arms of Grandma and Grandpa. What a fairyland. We immediately measured ourselves to see if we were taller than Grandma. She was just over five feet tall, so we accomplished that by fourth grade. We're a tall family.

The smell of their home is etched in my senses. When I recall it, a wave of peacefulness washes over me, even to this day. Grandma cooked a big dinner for us, which was the best food in the world, as far as I was concerned. Pork roast, meatloaf, mashed potatoes, gravy, and all the trimmings—the height of culinary pleasure. Our cousins were there to greet us, as they all lived in Ohio. I was always excited and happy to see them.

There was a small bubbling brook next to Grandma's house. One day my brothers, Tom and Jack, and my cousins,

Greg and David, and I walked along the bank and jumped from rock to rock in the shallow water. After going a couple blocks, we came across a bridge with hobos under it. We saw a fire with food being cooked on it and clothes hanging on the trees to dry. They were like creatures from another land. We remained hidden. We were convinced that if they saw us, they'd kidnap us. When our curiosity was sated, we turned around quietly and ran with great speed back to Grandma's.

As the sun was just starting to set, we went onto the large front porch that had a swing with chains attached to the ceiling. We sat on the swing if no adults were there. They had first choice. Finally, it became dark, and the hillside was lit with lightning bugs. It was our own show and we were thrilled. The moon was shining, the air was warm, stars were twinkling, and the lightning bugs flitted all around the field. What a spectacular moment.

We ran over to Grandma and asked her, "Can we please have some canning jars?" She gave them to us, and we proceeded to catch some of the lighting bugs. We all had our individual flashlights. After a couple of hours of fun, we were off to bed to get a good night's sleep. Sometimes our parents let us sleep on the porch, which was the icing on the cake.

The following morning I got up early and ran downstairs to the kitchen to see Grandma. I was convinced she slept there, if she slept at all. As I write this, I can smell the aroma of coffee. I hoped to be the chosen one to go to the store and get the rolls for breakfast. Grandma said the magic words while handing me a small amount of change.

"Mary Jean, will you get the rolls this morning?" Ecstatic, I skipped down the street on my important mission, arrived at the store, opened the door, which had bells on it to announce visitors, and entered. I stood in front of the penny-candy counter display, looked up at the owner, and said, "I'd like some rolls, please."

The owner of the store, seated behind the counter, looked at me and said, "You're Isabelle Gerard's daughter."

He was right, I thought he had magical powers to know that. I felt special. I got my order and returned to Grandma's. We sat and talked, and again, I felt special because it was just the two of us. My grandma was very important to me. She was a special person who loved me. Oh the joys of childhood!

* * *

CHAPTER 9

ONENESS/DEEKSHA

Renata called me one day in 2006 and asked, "Mary Jean, do you want to go with me to a Oneness/Deeksha seminar in Chicago, conducted by Ron Roth?"

I immediately asked, "What's that?"

She responded, "It's a spiritual movement, and I know it will further your spiritual growth. Spirit told me that you should attend this conference."

That's all I had to hear. I agreed to go. We both flew there, roomed together, and enjoyed the jubilation and positive messages that were disseminated. We were intrigued by the concepts. I thought about it periodically after that but didn't get further involved at that point.

I learned that the purpose of the Oneness Movement is to spread enlightenment and offer Divine Grace, known as Oneness Blessing/Oneness Deeksha. There's no organized religion involved. The way this grace is offered is that a Deeksha giver puts his or her hands on the top of one's head and lets them rest there from ten seconds to a minute so that the Divine light or energy can flow through. It's the transference of the sacred golden energy of Divine Grace, which descends, and initiates the recipient into higher states of consciousness.

Shortly after going to the Oneness/Deeksha seminar, I started thinking about moving to Asheville, North Carolina. I knew inwardly that it was an important leg of my journey. I discussed this with Renata, and she agreed. I'd been raised in Michigan, and some of my family and friends were there. Our house was like an enchanted cottage and gave us a great deal of pleasure. But my soul had to be someplace else, and I knew it. I was compelled to move to Asheville for the summer. No other city called to me.

I'd gone to Dr. George Goodheart (he introduced kinesiology to his fellow doctors and the public) for treatment and told him that I had this compulsion to move to Asheville, which I didn't understand.

He told me, "Consider it a gift." Dr. Goodheart was not only a superior doctor, but also very spiritual. He said, "Your spirit is leading you there."

Then I completely understood why I wanted to go. I knew it would help me heal. I was still struggling, so I made up my mind and told myself, I must move to Asheville.

People asked me if I knew anyone there, and I admitted that I didn't.

They'd ask, "How are you and Gerry going to work out being apart?

I would tell them, "We'll work it out." Gerry and I had long discussions about moving, and we did work it out. Our love is paramount.

Gerry was an adjunct professor at Wayne State University in Michigan and was teaching Philosophy of Education for the spring and summer terms. He retired from public school teaching in 1995, and teaching high school was his first love. He was an incredible teacher and still gets cards and calls from his former students. One of them at the university told him, "Teach until you die!"

After we commuted for two summers, it was finally time for him to say good-bye to teaching. He will always love teaching, but while he was working in Michigan, I became ill in Asheville and had to go to the hospital. He wanted to be with me if that were to happen again and was getting tired of the commute. He enjoyed visiting Asheville, so he agreed to move there, as he believed it was a good thing to do and very important to my quest for spirituality. I'm so grateful to him.

There are many activities we enjoy in Asheville. One of them happens every Friday night during the summer: drumming in the park. The park is bowl shaped, and on one side, there are rows of cement carved into it for seating. People with their bongo drums sit there, and drummers with large drums stand in the middle and lead all of the others as they all go along with the beat. They initiate the rhythm, others join in, and the crowd sways to the music.

People dance in the middle of the park. They don't join hands; there's simply free expression and abandonment. The only time there are two dancing as one is when a parent is holding a child in his or her arms or by the hands. It's a beautiful sight to behold. The air is warm, sometimes the moon is shining, and there's camaraderie among everyone. Throngs gather to be part of this event.

The first time I witnessed this wonderful gathering, I was enthralled. I'd never experienced anything like it. The rhythm of the beat went to the heart of my soul. I felt a connection to the other spectators, dancers, and drummers. I remember thinking at the time, no wonder the Indians danced around a campfire.

People have so much fun when they're expressing themselves and involved in a joyous gathering. And there's always something special and natural about being out in the open air. I always walk away with a lighter step. I love to see the faces of tourists, as there's a shining light in their eyes and happiness on their faces. They hear the drumming in the distance, follow the sounds, amble over, and join in. Asheville is such a special city, and I'm glad I was drawn here.

Another discovery was finding the Oneness/Deeksha Movement again. I was looking for a yoga studio and checked out three. I was drawn to one, called Namaste, stood in front of it, wondering if this was the one, and entered to check it out. It was perfect. Not only did they have great yoga, but I glimpsed a poster that said: "Oneness/Deeksha on Monday and Thursday nights."

I couldn't believe it. I wanted to experience it again, as I was still looking for help. The following Monday, I went. The room was filled with 25 people plus the Oneness/Deeksha givers. I received the blessing and walked out with the realization that I'd had a unique experience.

After receiving Oneness/Deeksha for three years, I experienced profound changes in my thinking. I didn't have to say affirmations; the change just happened. I decided I wanted to become a Deeksha giver and spent a weekend becoming one. I can now give the blessing to anyone who requests it.

The first time I gave Deeksha to a group was more than I expected. The old saying, "It's better to give than receive" is certainly true. There's a connection when I put my hands on each person's head; I feel an energy surge through me. I know I'm only a vehicle, but it's a privilege to be one and to help people change. I've seen physical and emotional changes in the people who attend Deeksha, and it's remarkable. Their eyes are brighter and clearer, and their demeanor is different. They are much more open and happy.

One time I hadn't gone to Deeksha for three weeks but suddenly said to Gerry, "I don't understand it, but I have this compulsion to go to Deeksha this Thursday." When I arrived, I found that a woman named Kathy, who is a very highly evolved awakened soul, was giving the Oneness blessing with the intent to connect with the Divine (to be awakened is to recognize fully our connection with the

Divine and with each other). People were anxious to have a Oneness Blessing from her because they knew how authentic she was. I'd never really connected with the Divine and yearned for that experience.

I was sixth in line and was patiently awaiting my turn with anticipation. Finally, my time arrived. Kathy put her hands on my head, and after a few seconds, I got the message telepathically: "The Divine is within you; all you have to do is recognize that. We all have a light inside of us, and we are all connected by cords." I had a hard time fully integrating the information.

Sheldon, one of the trainers, asked me, "Well, what do you think?"

I replied, "Well, I was told the Divine is within me."

He quietly responded with a lovely smile on his face, "Yes."

But I struggled during the following week because I wanted to believe, but I fought it.

Kathy came back the following Thursday, and I went to see her again. Immediately afterward, she put her hands on my head, and I silently asked again, "What is the Divine?"

I was told, "I told you before—the Divine is within you. You have all the answers within; all you have to do is ask. You have seen the Akashic records; you have the knowledge. You know, you have to trust. The Divine is within you." I got up and felt clearer than when I'd knelt down.

The Akashic Records (Akasha is a Sanskrit word meaning "sky" or "space") refers to records that contain all knowledge of human experience and the history of the cosmos. These records are stored on a different plane of existence. They're also referred to as a "library"; other analogies refer to a "universal supercomputer." It is asserted that the records update automatically and that they can be accessed through astral projection or when someone is placed under deep hypnosis.

In Edgar Cayce's book The Law of One, Book 1, which is said to contain conversations with a channeled "social memory complex" known to humans as "Ra," when the questioner asked where Cayce received his information, the answer was: "We have explained before that the intelligent infinity is brought into intelligent energy from eighth density or octave." Cayce used this gateway to experience the Akashic Records.

In Future Life Reading, author Helen Stewart Wambach, Ph.D. (1925–1985), who lived in Concorde, California, claimed to be able to read the Akashic Records. She said she could hypnotize people and enable them to experience their possible future lives in various alternative universes.

The whole concept was fascinating to me, and I was 75 percent convinced. But since I'm basically a doubting Thomas, I needed more proof. Fortunately for me, Anette Carlstrom, who was trained at the Oneness University in India and is referred to as Sweden's answer to the Dalai Lama, was lecturing and giving the Oneness blessing for one night at the University of North Carolina (UNC). I went with great anticipation. I loved doing anything that could further my spiritual growth.

Up to the podium came this angelic-looking creature with beautiful blonde-white wavy hair, very fair skin, and a flowing white dress. I was absorbed by what she had to say as she talked about the Oneness Blessing and how she found her spirituality. She then did some chanting and gave blessings. After she gave me a blessing, she put her hands over my palms, and I instantly felt the middle of my hands vibrate. I was so grateful. When I meditate or give the Oneness Blessing, the middle of my hands become quite warm and have a vibrating sensation, and I'm able to go deeper into others' blessings. I feel a strong connection to them.

Anette broadcasts over the internet and reaches people all around the world. It was one broadcast in particular that resonated with me. It was about embracing the Divine within and how that can change our lives. I still needed help with that.

Anette said, "Go to the place where you meditate, set up an altar with precious objects on it, and ask the Divine for help. Be sure and give thanks for all that the Divine has done previously."

I decided to try it. Every day I asked, "Please help me, and thank you for all that has been done for me." Jubilation! It worked. I was no longer a "Doubting Thomas." I now know that If I trust and listen, I can find the answers because they truly are within me. The more I listen and the more I trust, the easier life becomes. I had a shift in my thinking; my perceptions weren't the same. It was almost like seeing a movie and then getting new information that explains the movie and then perceiving it differently. This was a huge step in my recovery.

Part of my shift was that I started believing in reincarnation. I had doubts for many years but became convinced that we've all lived other lifetimes. It was the only thing that made sense to me. I respect if others don't agree with that philosophy because I can understand why they don't. It's difficult to accept anything other than what we can see; it's hard to grasp that we've been in different bodies.

But I had an experience that definitely made a believer out of me. While vacationing in Greece with Gerry, we were in an art gallery with whitewashed walls. We were looking at the art when suddenly I couldn't see out of my left eye. I thought the problem lay in my glasses, so I took them on and off until finally the eye was okay. It happened a couple more times when we were in Greece, but only for a moment.

After we returned home, I had problems with my eye periodically, but each episode got worse. I was quite concerned. One morning I had such pain in my eye and was so sick to my stomach that I knew I had to see an eye specialist. I was told that I had ocular migraines. The doctor told me, "You'll get sick to your stomach when they come on. Lie in bed until they pass." I accepted the diagnosis.

I'd gone to Dr. John Upledger for years, who was the developer of CranioSacral Therapy. I started going because of a TMJ problem that had plagued me for quite a while. Over time, I'd sought many treatments to relieve my pain but had little success. I'd been wearing a splint in my mouth for months. I used it when I exercised and when I slept. It was quite cumbersome, but I was willing to try anything.

A relative worked for Dr. Upledger and recommended him highly. I finally decided to see him, but with some reluctance. After all, no other doctor had helped me. I arrived the day of the appointment hopeful, but not too hopeful, because I didn't want to be disappointed again.

Dr. John walked into the room, and I started to tell him about what had happened to me. He interrupted and said, "Don't tell me anything." I was lying flat on my back on his table, and he picked up the heels of my feet and assessed my body. He lowered my feet back to the table and proceeded to the head of the table and put the palms of his hands under the back of my head. He then told me, "You have been hit either on the top of your head or underneath your jaw. Your palate had been pushed back and I will realign it." He did so, and I immediately felt better.

I was elated! Finally I'd found someone who could help me. I never wore the splint again. That was the beginning of Dr. John taking me down the path of health. He was an incredible friend, and I will always be eternally grateful to him.

I went to see Dr. John a couple times a year, which I called my "tune-up." During one session, he asked, "How are you doing?"

I replied, "I'm dealing with guilt. My mother is ill, and I find that I'm helping her because I don't want to feel guilty after she leaves. I loved helping my father during his last days on this planet, so I'm conflicted."

Dr. John said, "Relax and see what comes into your head." I closed my eyes and tried to clear my head as he was treating me with CranioSacral. I knew Dr. John believed in past lives, and he was a healer who had the ability to assist with these experiences.

All of a sudden, in my head I saw a bright, shiny, large, round gold shield. It was a strange moment—almost as if a movie were going on. I told Dr. John, and he said, "Look through the shield and tell me what is beyond that."

I kept saying. "I can't see anything."

He insisted, "Just keep looking."

I said. "I'm crazy to be coming up with all of this."

He replied, "Don't judge yourself; just go with what you're experiencing."

All of a sudden I could see beyond it. I said, "I see a man dressed in a short outfit with shoes that lace up the bottom part of his leg. He's standing next to the shield."

Dr. John said, "Tell me what's happening."

I answered, "I'm a slave girl dressed in a long blue dress, standing in front of this man, pleading for my release. I'm telling him that a young aristocratic man wants to marry me, but I know that 'you, my master, have to release me.' I'm waiting for his answer. 'No!' comes out of his mouth."

I continued: "I'm dejected and I have to get away. I will always be his slave. I cannot live with this unhappiness . . . I sneaked out late that night to meet my love. We are running through beautiful fields of high grasses with a few olive trees sprinkled about. The moon is lighting up the sky. We are ecstatic. We hear horses in the background, and now they're upon us. Sitting on them are men sent by the master to return me to the palace. They grab me, pull me onto one of the horses, and then brutally behead my love in front of my eyes. I'm screaming and crying and am fighting them. 'Put me down, put me down. You have killed my love.'

"One of the men fastens me with his strong arms, and on horseback takes me back to the master's residence. I am thrown into a room with just a bed in it, and all of the walls are whitewashed. I am terrified and in shock. My slave master comes to visit with jewels in his hands and exquisite fabrics that could be made into beautiful dresses for me and says, 'You could have had all of this if you had not disobeyed me.' He motions to another man in the room, who is holding a sword. All of a sudden I feel great pain because this despicable man stabs me in the left eye. I am bleeding profusely, and then he throws me out into the street."

I stopped talking at that point. I was worn out, but elated that I'd had my first past-life recollection.

I saw Dr. John a couple of months later, and he asked me, "Have you had any more past-life experiences?"

I answered, "Well, maybe, but there's a problem—I don't have any confirmation pertaining to them."

He exclaimed "Confirmation! When will you learn that you don't have to clearly understand something when it happens? After all, you talk on the phone, but you don't have to understand how the voice gets from one place to another."

That made sense to me, but I still had doubts.

About three months after seeing Dr. John, I said to Gerry, "I haven't had one problem with my eye since my past-life experience." I definitely made the connection between the two. I also realized that the past life took place in Greece, and I had been thrown into a room with whitewashed walls.

I've never had a problem with my eye since. My doubts were erased.

I find now that I can close my eyes and be in a different world than when I open them. When I was little, my mother would tell us that if we didn't go to sleep, a man would come in and take things from us or grab us. That would terrify me. I would close my eyes to make it go away, and it would, even if only temporarily.

Everything looks different in the dark than it does in the daylight. Finding out from Oneness/Deeksha that the Divine is within me brought a peacefulness to me. It took the fear away. And experiencing a past life made me realize how fleeting this lifetime is. The light is there all the time, and I can access the answers. I believe we all have a light inside us and are connected like light bulbs on a string.

* * *

CHAPTER 10

MY FATHER, GEORGE W. DRESBACH

The two words I would use to describe my journey so far are persistence and determination—determination to go forth, and the persistence to look at my life. After Forrest left, I told myself, "You can do it, you can do it." That helps me to keep going.

Sometimes I still feel like I'm in a maze, although the agony is beginning to lift, and the sun is beginning to shine again. I'm not trudging with heavy feet, but am beginning to walk with lightness. I'm finding out that simple pleasures in life are truly the best.

Renata is a constant stabilizing force in my life. My favorite times are when Forrest and Dad come in to talk. My father was the most important person to me when I was growing up. I have wonderful memories of him that I'll never forget. I remember when I was a little girl standing on the heat register in the morning in a cold house. Our coal furnace had to be stoked every morning for the coals to ignite and throw off heat. I felt so warm and safe while standing there. My dad would be the one to go down to the basement, shovel coal from the coal bin into the coal furnace, and get the fire going. I always knew that my dad could and would take care of me.

Other moments of joy were also linked to my dad. He taught me how to swim, ride a bike, drive a car (before drivers' training), and how to dance. Oh, how I loved to dance with Dad! I felt like I was gliding on air. He was always happy, enjoyed all kinds of music, and loved us beyond belief. His arms were a safe tent for me to run to. He was consistent, and I could count on that.

Dad was my beacon, my mast in the storm. It was stormy most of the time while growing up, as I never knew who my mother would be. Would she be the angry mother, the distant mother, the critical mother, the unloving or unaffectionate mother? I was overwhelmed by feelings of abandonment. Dad was the peacekeeper; his love permeated the house. He kept the family together, and his love sustained me.

When I think about my father, sometimes I ask myself, What is a successful life? I wonder about that at times. I know it depends on one's definition of success. I don't think it should be defined by worldly accoutrements such as job status, amount of money earned, or the kind of car one drives. My dad was a very successful man, but he didn't earn what is considered big money in his lifetime. His love and care for his family were paramount to him. He helped us in any way he could.

Dad had a serious heart attack in his latter years, but the crisis passed, and on one particular evening, the doctors told my brothers and me to go home and get some rest, which we did. The phone rang early the next morning, and a nurse said, "Come immediately. Your dad had a serious cardiac arrest." I raced to the hospital; and in the meantime, the doctors shocked his heart back, and it started working properly.

I talked to Dad afterward, and he told me what had happened while the doctors were working on him. He said, "I went into a beautiful, bright white light and found supreme happiness and peace that I hadn't experienced before. All of my worldly stresses were gone. I was told telepathically that I wasn't finished on Earth, and that I should go back because it wasn't my time to go."

He accepted that and went back into his body. I was fascinated and amazed by his experience. I'd read about this happening to other people, but this was my dad, and it became real for me. I was thrilled that he'd glimpsed the other side and experienced its peacefulness. It was the first time I became aware that he had stresses and struggles like all of us. He handled situations with calmness and patience, so I could never imagine his psyche having stress. He always made the choice to handle it, and not let it handle him. I found out it was his choice. What a great lesson to learn.

At the end of my father's stay on this planet, he was lying in a hospital bed, very ill with cancer and a serious heart condition. The doctors continued to be optimistic and told the family not to worry. I was there visiting him one evening and had the strange feeling that he was ready to go when I walked into his room. We had a wonderful visit, and I was reluctant to leave.

Finally, I decided he needed some rest and that I should go. His dark eyes looked at me, and I felt that they were filled with the knowledge that he wouldn't be here for long. I immediately went back three more times, kissed him, and said, "I love you, Dad. You're a wonderful father."

His eyes haunted me. There was no sadness in them, just peace. But I left with apprehension. He did leave the following morning, alone. I was devastated that I hadn't been at his side when he left and that I didn't follow my inner guide, which told me he was leaving.

Three months after my dad left this planet, my late husband, two of our best friends, and I visited other close friends in England to celebrate my 50th birthday. I received a birthday gift from two of my relatives, who sent me to a well-known psychic named Doris Collins. Doris had a wonderful reputation for talking to the other side. In fact, she was actor Peter Sellers' psychic.

My two girlfriends and I drove to her house, sat down, and waited for her. The door to the office opened, and a very tall, buxom, motherly woman walked into the room and announced who she was. Doris took me into her private office and said, "Maybe who you want to come in will, and maybe they won't."

I was there to talk to my father, so I knew that I'd be incredibly disappointed if I didn't hear from him. But I wasn't disappointed. He came in immediately and talked about the last night he had been alive. He told me through Doris, "I died alone, and that was okay. I saw you come back three times, looking anguished. Please don't feel bad; that's how I wanted it. There are flowers surrounding me, there is great beauty here, and I am peaceful."

Before he left, he said, "Tell your mother that Ruth is here."

I said to Doris, "The name Ruth doesn't mean anything to me. My mom and dad didn't have any friends or relatives by that name." When I left the room, my eyes were filled with tears.

When I saw my friends, one said, "Well, we don't have to ask if your dad came in."

After returning home, I told my mother, "I saw a medium while I was in England. Dad came in and said, 'Tell your mother that Ruth is here.'"

She answered, "Your father was going with Ruth when I met him. He must be very unhappy where he is." I chuckled to myself and was amazed by that information. I accepted the possibility that what had been said to me by Doris was possible, but I wasn't completely convinced. I realize today that it was accurate.

* * *

I wanted to be like my dad. He didn't hurt people; and he was safe, kind, and grounded. My mother always talked about how her children loved their father more than they loved her. There was truth in that statement, especially for the four oldest. Dad reached out and gave of himself with love and compassion. It was the pleasure of giving that was important to him. He didn't give love with conditions. There were no strings attached.

My life was happy when he was around, as love was part of his inner fiber. He was tall, with dark hair and eyes; and he loved music, fishing, hunting, and being with his children. My mother cast a shadow; whereas my father emanated a loving, healing light. I'm eternally thankful that my father was in my life. He brought happiness to me the whole time he was on this planet, and then from the other side. Was he born that way, or did he develop his kind demeanor? I think he was born that way, and as he grew, so did his wonderful qualities.

I didn't shed tears as a child. I was told by my dad, "Big girls don't cry." Crying was a definite no-no. For years I didn't cry. Forrest said to me at my father's funeral, "Mom, you're so strong." He knew how much I loved Dad, and yet I didn't shed one tear. I was conditioned not to cry, and I'd learned how to control the flow of tears. I felt tremendous loss and sorrow, but I felt I had to be stoic.

That started to change after Dad's parting, but I was embarrassed if tears came. They gave me a headache, as my tears seemed to be caught somewhere, locked up forever. After Forrest left, they became unlocked; the tears tumbled down my face, and I couldn't control them. In a short time, I was no longer embarrassed.

Today, I have no problem crying; I don't have to hide my feelings. It's such a relief to allow a natural reaction to take place. Sometimes the floodgates open, and the tears just gush forth. It's a good feeling and a natural occurrence.

When I think of Dad, I run into his safe arms. There was a special feeling being in his arms, and I can still feel them around me. My eyes fill with tears as I remember, but they're tears of happiness. My dad gave me so much. Thank you, Dad.

* * *

Renata went to Indiana to visit her brother and sister-in-law for Christmas. She had a bite on the back of her leg, which caused her concern. It happened while she was in Florida and didn't seem to be getting any better. She called me and said, "My leg was really bothering me this morning. I asked my brother, Tom, and sister-in-law, Sue, to look at my leg. They said the area had become very enlarged and red. They immediately took me to the hospital. A wound specialist was called in and he said, 'The bite seems to be from a brown recluse spider; unattended it could be deadly.'"

She was treated twice a week, but her health continued to deteriorate. She ended up having a gall bladder operation, bypass heart surgery, and lung surgery. She also suffered from diabetes and had kidney failure. She spent three days a week on dialysis.

Renata told me, "I get so sick from the dialysis, but I need it. It's hard for me to keep my strength. Forrest came in last night and gave me a jolt of energy that lifted me up off of my chair. You'll be surprised to find out who Forrest is, but the time isn't right now." Two weeks later, she called and said excitedly, "I'm on a waiting list for a kidney."

What wonderful news! I believed that my mentor, spiritual mother, and dear friend would survive her ordeal.

Renata had taken the final tests for her kidney transplant. A young man she'd been counseling offered her his kidney.

He said, "You saved my life, so I want to save yours."

She was in great spirits and so thankful. I talked to her on a Thursday, and she said, "I'm going in front of the board tomorrow to find out when I'll have my transplant. I'll call you tomorrow." I went to bed, anticipating good news the following day.

* * *

CHAPTER 11

LETTERS TO RENATA

That night, July 30, 2010, the phone rang at 12:31 a.m. I ran to answer it, half asleep, hoping it was a wrong number, because, if not, I knew it would be terrible news. I warily said, "Hello."

It was Renata's brother, Tom. I knew something was wrong. He told me, "Renata passed away today."

All I could say was, "Oh, no, oh no." I couldn't believe it, yet it was really happening.

Tom said, "Renata took her dog, Izzie, for a walk, sat down at a picnic table, and fell over onto the ground. A neighbor saw Izzie running around in distress and called the police. EMS arrived but couldn't revive her."

I said, "I'm so sorry, I'm so sorry." I couldn't get any other words out.

Tom said, "She's gone through so much. I was sure she would get a new kidney and be healthy." My heart went out to him.

I can't remember the rest of the conversation; I was in a daze. We said our good-byes, and I told him I'd call him the next day. I put down the phone and went back to the bedroom with such a heavy heart.

I was crying as I told Gerry about the conversation. "Renata, my beloved friend and teacher, is gone." He cradled me in his arms.

* * *

Everyone mourns in their own way. Some people wail in agony, some people cry in private and put on a different face in public, some people recognize the suffering of individuals before they leave this planet and are able to be happy they're out of pain and misery, and some think only of their own loss. I was a combination: glad that Renata had escaped from her pain, but desperately feeling her loss. I felt selfish because I wished she were still here so I could pick up the phone and talk to her. I was only thinking of myself, but I couldn't seem to get past that.

I called Tom the next day and asked. "What are the funeral arrangements? I'm so sorry, but we're unable to attend. However, can we help with the cost of the funeral? I feel so helpless. Please, let me do that."

He graciously agreed. I sent a letter to be read, if possible, at the service:

> "Goodbye for now, my beautiful friend. Life will never be the same without you, but you have spun gold around my life. I bow my head and heart to you as I continue on my journey. It will be lonelier without you, but only for a while. You will touch me from the other side. I will never forget you. How can I?

> You are woven into my thoughts. I will listen for what more you have to teach me. You made me a better person. Our paths were meant to cross."

After the service, Tom called and said, "The service was small and beautiful. I gave a great tribute to her."

I find myself wondering what Renata would think of my way of mourning. I believe that she would have compassion for me and understand. While I was going through that dark period, I remembered what she'd taught me. I recognized her incredible teaching abilities. The patience alone that she had was phenomenal. We peeled the onion together to get to the core of issues. She never became impatient, no matter how long it took. She only offered encouragement and then joy when an issue was resolved.

How could I not miss such a rare presence on this planet? I determined that I'd be kind to myself during this transition—Renata taught me that. After all, tears come while peeling an onion. That's just how it is.

A beautiful light left this planet—one who only gave and never took. She helped many people who were suffering. She was a rare person whose rewards lay in helping others, quietly but successfully. She didn't need worldly acclaim, although she certainly deserved it.

I know that all individuals have worth, but her value to me was immeasurable. I cry as I write this; the loss is just so profound. I will live her message—that will be my greatest tribute to her.

Here are some letters I wrote to her after her passing:

> August 8, 2010
> Dear Renata,
>
> It has been 3 three days since you left. There is a huge void in my life. You were in Indiana and I am in Asheville, but the vacuum spreads everywhere. You touched my life so

profoundly. You enabled me to grow, my hand in yours. You connected me to Forrest, my dad, and others on the other side. You opened doors that I could never have on my own. You were always there urging gently for me to go forth into new territory. I can feel your presence as I write this. You reassured me that I could attain a different consciousness. We had such in-depth conversations and you knew me completely. You always liked what you saw. I was gifted with a loving friend.

I am challenged to call on what you taught me, I know you are happy where you are. You didn't have an easy life here, but you kept going, helping people to get through their lives. Your capacity to give to others was limitless. You always thought of others, not yourself. Your animals were your children. I remember how you preferred to stay home on Thanksgiving. You cooked dinner and then fed your beloved animals some of it. You even gave them pumpkin pie and whipped cream. They loved it, and it was exactly where you wanted to be.

I learned a great deal about you over the years, and I liked all that I learned. I admired and respected you. You were a strong and steady voice. Your intellect was high and you had a thirst for knowledge. You especially leaned toward the American Indian culture. I will never be able to replace you, and I never want to. Your energy is so strong that it will reach me again. I have patience, I know it will happen. After all, I learned this from you. Someday I will be meditating or sitting quietly and you will come to me. That keeps me going.

August 16, 2010
Dear Renata,

Another week and one day has gone by and no Renata to talk to. No Renata to go to for answers. I am constantly aware of the loss. I can almost feel you, but not quite. I don't want anyone to fill the space you were in, you are irreplaceable. I feel your arms around me comforting my soul. Life is a little harder without you.

I cling to the knowledge that you are happy where you are. I know the last thing you would want is for me to be unhappy. You would tell me I have the strength to continue to grow. That was your gift to me. Time heals all wounds. Mine is still wide open and raw. It will close as time goes on. It's all too new. My emotions are fragile and I honor that.

You touched so many people. Your kindness and love is embedded in them. My soul bursts with love and gratitude for you. This awareness will start the healing process. You always said, "Accept things as they are, not how you want them to be." I'm trying, I'm trying.

August 30, 2010
Dear Renata,

It's been one month since you left, and it's Forrest's birthday. I hope the two of you are together. I miss you terribly, my dear, sweet friend. It's painful not to be able to hear your comforting voice. I hear it by memory but it is not the same. I go about my day and there is a void. The loss is multifaceted—on so many levels. You came onto this planet to help people, and you did. You told me the story of when you were a little girl and your grandfather was lying in bed dangerously ill in your home. You said, "Mother, Grandpa is going to leave soon." Your mother didn't want to hear that, so you went outside and sat on the porch steps. While you were there, your grandpa came to you and said, "Good-bye." You went into the house because you knew he was gone, and he was. That was the beginning of a life having contact with the other side. A precious gift that you shared with me and others."

You got an education—in fact, received a master's degree. You had struggles in a marriage and finally left because your husband was an alcoholic and he wouldn't do anything about it. You moved to Florida and started seeing clients. You were an intuitive counselor. The best as far as I am concerned. You could see energy fields and pick out my problems and then help me with them. You were always sure I could handle them before you enlightened me about them. Your common sense was boundless. I have never met anyone who has so much spiritual knowledge.

I remember the day when you called me and said, "Forrest came to me and asked me to call you because it was your birthday." I was elated because it was. You told me once that you could not make all of this up. You didn't have the kind of memory required to remember what the spirits said previously. I understood, after all, you have many clients. How could you remember all that? I've learned so much from you, my precious friend.

> "I love you, Renata. I will never forget you. Now I can look up at the stars at night and know you are looking down at me. You're probably hanging around with Forrest and my dad. You all are the greatest company.
>
> Love on, my friend. I know this is the way it is supposed to be.

I still talk to Renata every day. If a problem arises, I ask, "How would Renata handle it?" I always get the answer. Forrest said to me many times, "Mom, I am only a thought away." It is so comforting to know I have helpers who love me and want to help me. I am never alone; they are always there. I accept that fully. All I have to do is ask.

The answer isn't in Earth language; it comes as a feeling. I simply know what to do. At one time in my life I would have worried about what people would think about this. But no longer. I've had many confirmations. My life on this planet has been changed because of help from Forrest and Dad on the other side. Their wisdom and advice has helped me shed the old and embrace the new. Actually, compassion, acceptance, and nonjudgement aren't new concepts for me. They've just been stored away for a while. Forrest and Dad, along with Renata, helped me get them out of storage.

It was easy to love Renata; many people did. She helped so many, and I know that's true because I've talked to some of them. They rave about her abilities and how she changed their lives. My husband is a philosopher, and at times is a doubter, but he said, "She was one of the most insightful therapists I've ever encountered. She had an insight and intuitiveness that made her excellent."

Renata was brilliant and had help from the other side. She told me, "I connect with spirit, and spirit gives me the answers."

Most of the time she didn't remember what we'd discussed before, and by that I mean the details. She said,

"I don't keep notes." She had the best notetaker there was, and that was spirit. Spirit remembered; she didn't have to.

I realize that it was a rare privilege to have been counseled by Renata, and I will be eternally grateful. She said, "It was a joy for me, also, and that was because you worked diligently to change." There is no alakazam or magic to changing. I made the decision that I wanted to learn new ways of living my life, and Renata led the way.

Some types of perception changing took a long time. A good example is my relationship with my mother, but it was so worth it. Renata was and is my spiritual mother. In Australia there's a musical instrument called the didgeridoo. It takes study and expertise to master that instrument. Similarly, I've found that it took time for me to take up the instrument of change. But I had so much help along the way. My instructors were so loving and caring.

I compare my life before Renata to a huge hole that was being dug in the ground, with garbage being dumped into it. The garbage may have been hidden, but it was still there. My body and mind were dumping grounds for toxic material, and I didn't know how to get rid of it.

Renata told me, "It will eventually make you physically ill." She helped me take it out piece by piece and examine it. When I realized I didn't need to keep it, I was able to get rid of it. It took a long time to be free of the poison, but I know it will not return. Occasionally I find a little residue, but I throw it away immediately. My body is no longer a dumping ground.

Renata always said, "Learn from wisdom, not woe." Her wisdom was boundless. She came in with much knowledge and constantly learned more while she was here. She loved the native Indian culture and their wisdom that had been passed down.

She passed on a quote from a Sioux called Black Elk: "The first peace, which is the most important, is that which comes within the souls of people when they realize their relationship, their oneness, with the Universe and all its powers, and when they realize that at the center of the Universe dwells the great Spirit, and that their center is really everywhere. It is within each of us."

Mother nature was important to Renata. She respected the earth and all who reside on the planet. Knowledge gained is knowledge earned. I want to learn something through wisdom every day.

I am holding a special crystal from Renata. I can feel the good, pure energy she put into it. It energizes and calms me at the same time. What a wonderful world to supply us with crystals! I feel strongly about protecting Mother Earth. She provides us with all we take for granted: the air to breathe, water to drink, trees to clean the air, flowers with sweet fragrance, medicines from the rain forest to heal us, energy to keep us cool or warm, food that feeds us, the materials to build our homes, beautiful mountains to behold and hike on, seas and lakes to swim in.

We put boats in the water to get from one destination to another and to get a supply of fish. I look to the sky every night I can and thank the universe for the sun, the moon, and all that it provides. I thank Mother Earth for her benevolence. I want to be kind to her because she is so kind to me. She never asks for anything in return; she just keeps giving. How can I not honor her? It is my privilege to do so.

I've been depressed off and on since Renata left this planet. Not only is she gone, but my contact with Forrest and my dad are gone. It's almost like losing Forrest again; in fact, it is losing him again. There was such comfort in talking to Renata, who was so wise, and then Forrest and Dad through her. I have to trust that I will have contact with them again. It is only a matter of time. I am very sad; it's such a tremendous loss. My eyes fill with tears and a lump forms in my throat as I think about it. I welcome the tears as they wash away the grief.

I'm familiar with this feeling. I like other feelings more, but this is how it is for the moment. I'll remember the joy and wonderful times I had with Renata. She was one of the most important people in my life. I will never forget her. I love her. I know that she sends her love to me. She isn't suffering anymore, and that means everything to me. I will wait patiently, and one day she will pop in. It will be a grand reunion. I can hardly wait.

* * *

Pictures of me and my loved ones

In Loving Memory of Arthur Forrest Tull II - August 30, 1957 - March 11, 1995.

From a past letter written by Arthur Forrest Tull, II, addressed, "Dear Family"

While under the pressures of coping with society, it is often difficult to really be aware of how great many things are.

I feel so lucky now that I can look at what we have and appreciate it. I am so proud to be a part of this family and I love you all. I often do not express my true feelings verbally because I find it difficult. But you can be assured I love you and am thankful you are a part of my life.

Love,
Forrest

Dad and Mom -Newly married, Detroit, MI,1928

My father, George W. Dresbach

Jack, Dad, Mom, Tom and me in Detroit, MI

My brothers, The Dresbach Men -Jack, Jim, Tom and Kyle

Amidst my brothers, Jack, Tom and Kyle

Modeling picture of me taken at the Detroit Institute of Art for a special fashion section in the Detroit Free Press

Big brother Forrest, with his little sister, Valarie, in his favorite red wagon.

Forrest with our pet kitten.

Valarie with our pet kitten

Valarie at 12 years old and Forrest at 14.

Valarie and I in mother/daughter dresses, which I made.

Valarie and I in Paris.

Forrest in his 20's, during a healthy period

Modeling picture of Valarie

Robert at our former lake house in Michigan

Jonathan at a Detroit Tigers ballgame

Jackson, a great deal of fun

Gerry and I

Robert, Jonathan and I at my birthday party

Gerry and Valarie

Gerry and I in our boat in Michigan

The last picture taken of Forrest and me

PART II

Healing . . . And What I Learned

CHAPTER 12

WAKING UP

When I started to wake up from the nightmare I was living, I was more and more aware that I had to learn how to live differently. My life had changed drastically. No more Forrest. I had to pick up the pieces and see if they fit into where I was going. I knew I wanted to take a different path, but I just didn't know how.

I wanted to run away and leave my problems behind me. Maybe I could find someplace where my emotions and thinking would be rearranged. But I didn't know where that could be. Anyplace but here. That wouldn't be hard to find, would it? I could choose the location, anywhere in the world. It would be worry free—with no sorrow, no past, and no future—just happiness. Sounded like nirvana.

How soon could I leave? "Now! I can leave now! I'll pack and be on my way. But what about all of the good memories

I've accumulated? They aren't allowed there; sorrows aren't either. I don't want to leave all that behind. I have to find a new way."

I finally came to the realization that I needed something that would help me climb out of the hole of sadness I was in. I came across the following processes one by one and decided to call them my "tools." I started out with a few, and then added more as I found them. I created a "toolbox" to put them in, and it never leaves my side. Just as I had to learn to walk and talk as a baby, I learned to live my life as it is today by utilizing my tools.

My toolbox is my most valuable possession; without it my journey wouldn't have been possible. I can't physically see my toolbox, but it is there nevertheless. I imagine it to be a sky-blue box with lovely flowers painted all over it. It's lined in red velvet, has a small handle, and I can open it from the top.

Following are the tools that helped me change my life and find peace and happiness:

1. Stopped drinking
2. Meditation
3. Yoga
4. Acupuncture
5. Meeting Renata; Deeksha or the Oneness Blessing

Tools I leaned from Renata:

a. Acceptance—accept things as they are, not how I want them to be
b. Non-judgment
c. Compassion
d. Living in the moment
e. Our thoughts create our reality
f. Living in reality; not illusion—illusion creates confusion
g. Come from the heart, not the mind

My body actually shook at times during the long months after Forrest left. It reacted to the storm that ravaged my life. At times, I appeared to have a calmness embedded in me, but that was deceiving. My outside being told a different story than my inner being. The storm would abate, and then it would arise again out of nowhere.

At first, I wasn't prepared, but over time, I gathered the tools to help me deal with my emotional upheaval. I'm aware that another storm, maybe a typhoon, can slam me, but I now feel that I'll be able to handle it. That's a comfortable feeling. I'll never be stranded again. I may get soaked from the water, but I will survive. My tools are my raft.

After the storm, a tiny drop of rain glistened like a jewel on a beautiful lime-green leaf reaching out from the linden tree. It sat there only wanting to give the leaf a drink of water. Along my journey, there were glistening jewels always ready to help and nurture me. They were in my toolbox. Maybe I should have called it my jewel box.

Today, there's a flame I can visualize when I close my eyes. It doesn't become brighter or duller; it is constant and steady. It never even flickers. It's the flame of life that keeps me going no matter want the circumstances are. It's a reassuring light that tells me: "All is well."

I'm glad that I have that visualization. I know life will continue to present challenges, but with my toolbox and the light, I'm up to task of handling them. I carry my toolbox with me and also my light. I call it my own light bulb. I don't even have to switch it on. It's always there telling me that I can do it.

* * *

CHAPTER 13

MY TOOLBOX

Now I will go into more depth with respect to the items in my toolbox that helped me heal.

1. The first tool I used was to stop drinking. It was a small one, but not that easy. All of my friends and family drank, so I became the odd one in the crowd. However, we all adjusted in time. I found that I could enjoy myself without a drink, and I felt good in the morning. This was my tribute to Forrest. I stopped drinking on his birthday.

2. My next tool was meditation. I had thought about doing it throughout the years. I started meditating twice daily: 30 minutes in the morning, and 30 in the afternoon. I was

on my way. Life did take a turn for the better, as meditation made my days brighter. Forrest's leaving was a life-defining moment—little did I know how much it would change me. But his leaving propelled me forward.

Meditation calmed my mind, and peace descended over me. I cleared my mind and slowed down my thoughts, which brought calmness to my life. Sometimes I got answers to problems that I was trying to work out—they just arrived. I had the desire to change my thought patterns, and then I had to go about doing so.

Meditation caused me to question my beliefs: Who am I? What are my values? What do I think? I'd never thought about those questions until Forrest left. I was an accumulation of the teachings of my parents, educational upbringing, and religion. I never wanted to hurt people, and I follow the laws of the land, but deep down inside, I wondered: Who am I? How do I react to situations? Am I thoughtful? My path led me to investigate those questions. I didn't wake up one day and start to live differently. It was a gentle process, and it's ongoing,

I discovered a burning desire to be nonjudgmental, accepting, loving, and compassionate. It's as though I took my inner being out, looked at it, and replaced a great deal of it. My life has been enriched by this practice. After 13 years of meditation, I am more drawn to it than ever.

3. The third tool I used was yoga. It taught me how to breathe in order to be healthy, and to relieve stress. I use both deep breathing and alternate breathing. Alternate breathing balances both sides of the brain. It's a little more complicated, but very effective.

4. The fourth step I took was acupuncture. It facilitates the flow of prana, life force, throughout the body, and puts it in balance. My body and mind relaxed. I found out that

balance was a key way for me to help heal physical problems and emotional issues.

I pet Jackson, our cat, and he purrs with contentment. I pet myself with meditation, yoga, and acupuncture; and purr with contentment.

5. The next and most important tool was meeting Renata. I liken it to six huskies pulling a sled across the crusted frozen snow. Dark is approaching and they have to be at their destination by nightfall. The leader cracks his whip so that they speed up. The dogs give their all and plunge forward. In my case, I had a destination, although at one time I didn't know it. I was trudging across deep snow hoping I didn't fall through any unexpected openings. I was fearful, but I had to go on. I had to climb out of the mire of desperation and survive. The days were long and cold, and at times I just couldn't find warmth.

I knew that just one ray of sunshine could give me hope; that's what I needed in order to go on; and the long, cold road took a huge turn when I met Renata. She slowly stoked the fires with her wisdom until my entire being was filled with warmth. I bask in it now. The huskies reached their destination, also. They had a full meal and languished in front of a warm fire.

Renata was a counselor, friend, and medium who opened a whole new world for me. She took hours to help me learn new ways to live. She imparted words of wisdom, which helped me on my road to healing, which I will share in this chapter. She spent many sessions until I understood what they meant. I'm able to call on them today to help me through challenges. Renata was my main healer, and I would not be where I am today if it weren't for her.

All of the words Renata shared resonated with me, but I found this phrase the most useful, powerful, and also the hardest to accomplish:

"ACCEPT THINGS AS THEY ARE, NOT HOW YOU WANT THEM TO BE."

My desires would erupt, and I would want things to be as I wanted them to be. I didn't want to accept the fact that Forrest had left. I felt sorry for myself, and was bitter and depressed. I had many sorrowful feelings for a long time. I fought against reality, but finally I had to realize that acceptance was the answer. I had no control. No matter how hard I wished that things were different, they simply weren't.

Renata said, "If you continue to have those feelings, you will become physically ill." I realized I had to change my path, go in a different direction, and find peace. That was the only way to honor Forrest's life.

Life is like a play. There are acts, scenes, actors, and actresses. The only difference is that there's no script. My actions and reactions resulted from my early upbringing. In many ways, the acts and scenes were already written for me. I couldn't change them until I decided I didn't like the play. I wanted out of this one; I wanted to create a new act.

Today, most of the cast is the same, with new additions along the way. I am director, producer, stage manager, and casting director. I can start each day with "curtains up" and end with "curtains down." I go to bed and replenish my body and soul for the next act the following morning. I adjust the dialogue as I go through the day. Shakespeare said, "All the world's a stage and the men and women merely players." I understand what he meant. My current life embodies a different perspective from the one I had in the past, and the truth lies within it.

* * *

The two hardest things I had to deal with in my life were my relationship with my mother and my son leaving. There's nothing that compares to Forrest leaving, but I find it amazing that his leaving allowed me—through communicating with him on the other side—to come to terms with my mother. I accept her now. I know that she did the best she could with the tools she had at the time.

Before I came to that realization, I had to examine my early relationship with my mother, but it was an area I didn't want to delve into. I knew I carried guilt because she wasn't able to give me love. She could care for me physically but not love me with words and touch. I always felt it was my fault that the relationship didn't work. I felt guilty and angry at the same time. Often, those feelings came out inappropriately.

One of the confusing aspects of my life while I was growing up was why my mother was so different when she was out in public. She put a mask on when she walked out the door. She was friendly to people and smiled a lot. But then she would take off her mask when she entered our home.

I know now that I can't go into her psyche. I can only accept things as they happen. It was all part of my journey. Do I love my mother? Yes, I do. And I could never have made that statement ten years ago. Do I like the way she treated me? No. I will never be able to recall Hallmark moments with her, but that's okay. If I constantly dreamed about the ways in which I wanted her to be different from how she was, I knew that I would be stuck in a desire that would never be fulfilled.

My mother came in a few times during my sessions with Renata. She apologized, saying, "No human being should be treated the way I treated you." My heart wasn't open at first. I listened to her, but I couldn't forgive. The hurt was still raw, an open sore. But as time went on and as I examined my entire life with her, my heart opened little by little. It took months until I could forgive her. I wasn't condoning the physical and emotional pain, but I was able to eventually forgive.

I'm now grateful that she brought me into this planet. I still don't like how she treated me, but I'm free from the hurt and pain. I'm able to live my life without being tainted with thoughts from my former perspective.

Renata told me, "Give it all back to her." So I did. In fact, I started to feel sorry for my mother because of how unhappy she was and all that she'd missed out on.

I no longer look at my mother in the same way. She didn't change, but my perception of her did. I still don't like how she treated me, but I understand now why she did it, and I forgive her. I will never condone her behavior, but I realize that she was clinically depressed and her life didn't turn out the way she had envisioned it to be. After my dad passed away, she took antidepressants and was a different person. Unfortunately, she only took them for a short time, and after stopping, she reverted back to her old patterns.

However, I eventually healed my long-held painful feelings. I know now that my perception as a young child that it was all my fault wasn't true. I no longer carry that burden and shadow. It flew away, never to return.

* * *

With Forrest, I use the analogy of a chair sitting in the middle of a room. It is empty, never to be used again by the person who left. When Forrest left, a void appeared that could never be filled again. No one could take his space; it was only for him. But I came to see that life could unfold with great unhappiness. I learned how to change unhappy to happy. At one time I would have thought that would be impossible. The transfer for me was from unhappy to acceptance. That chair will always be empty, but Forrest will always live in my heart.

Looking back, I can understand that after Forrest left, I wasn't able to look forward; the mist was too heavy. I'd never been in that territory before. The grief and pain clouded all of my thoughts and feelings. It was a dark time, and I couldn't get up.

But I finally did what I didn't think was possible: I got up. Do I wish Forrest were here? Of course I do, but that's not possible. A big part of my healing stems from the fact that I know he's happy where he is. Thanks to being able to communicate with him through Renata, I was able to know the truth of that. He wasn't happy at the end of his life on this planet, so I knew that I'd be incredibly selfish to wish him back under those circumstances. He was the one who suffered 24 hours a day. He was in pain. I didn't experience what he did. I had to remember that when I got desperate.

To accept things as they are and not how I wanted them to be didn't mean I didn't have an intent. My intent was to do what I could to influence positive outcomes and then give it up. Drs. George Goodheart and John Upledger, two men who were my physicians and friends, told me that they wrote on a piece of paper what they wanted to accomplish, then they folded up the paper, put it in a drawer, and forgot about it. The result they asked for always happened.

Now, the rhythm of life is not always upbeat, but I can hold my baton and direct what kind of music I like. I can create my own symphony.

My mantra was: "Looking good. Looking good. Do I look good? You look good." The exterior seemed so important. If I looked good, others would notice me and that meant that I was okay. I realize now what a fallacy that was. I made my living by looking good. My tools at that time were makeup, hair styles, how I walked down the runway, dressing fashionably, and being the best I could be physically. I constantly judged myself and others. One of the hardest things to do was to look into the shadow, where all the repressed emotions from childhood were, take them out, and release them one by one.

At first, I was afraid to open that box of shadows, but I finally did with Renata by my side. There was nothing to be afraid of. It was like cleaning out the attic. Now, the attic is clear and the box is empty. I accept myself as I am, My doubts about myself were erased by accepting that I am fine the way I am. Acceptance 101.

Do I consider other people's feelings? Do I take into consideration why they act the way they do? Are they physically and mentally well? Before, I only thought of how others' behaviors affected me. Not how it affected them. I've found that some people justify their actions by how the world treats them. They were hurt as children and brought in issues from past lives, or they're just having a bad day. There are a myriad of reasons why people act the way they do. Same for me. I no longer carry the burden of relying on others to find my worth. I found it right where it was all the time: within me.

I want to really know people rather than just see an illusion. That type of acceptance brings about a different person. It's like putting on glasses and seeing the real person for the first time. They're like magic glasses, but not really; they're glasses of reality. To see the real people is the only way to enjoy them. Whatever their quirks, that's okay. They're just different from me. That's what it's all about. Differences rather than sameness. There are different paintings, and I can enjoy all of them. Why not people?

Seeing out of my eyes now, the world is a more beautiful place. I started to see more beauty as soon as I accepted how things really are. There's a wonder to my life now that I accept how my life will unfold. And that's what this journey is all about.

A storm is coming; batten down the hatches. Prepare for the worst. I've done that in my life. No chance that it could be a mild rainstorm or a lovely mist falling from the sky. In my mind, it could only be terrible. I did that after Forrest left. Every phone call was a siren warning me of danger, danger! I was waiting expectantly for the next fatal storm.

I wasn't even conscious of what I was doing. It was a new way of living for me. My senses were on alert, just waiting.

Because of Renata, I found out that I didn't have to anticipate tragedy. It took a long time to get over that way of thinking. First I had to recognize what was happening, and then I had to go to work to change it. Acceptance wasn't easy, but it was worth it.

Thank you, Renata.

* * *

CHAPTER 14

LESSONS FROM RENATA

I tried to extricate myself from the confusion I felt for years. Not that I would be immersed in that state constantly, but if a stressful situation would arise, I would immediately go back to those feelings. I didn't like being there, and some aspects were frightening, but I wasn't sure how to get out. And I wondered, will I ever get out? I had to ask the question before I could look for the answer.

"ILLUSION CREATES CONFUSION. CONFUSION CREATES HAVOC. ILLUSION IS THERE TO FIND OUT WHAT IS REAL."

Confusion arose when I didn't look at reality correctly and let illusion take over. There's illusion in movies and music, which is a great part of their appeal. They attempt to make illusion look like the truth. But I knew that if I looked at a situation and tried to make potatoes out of squash, I had a problem. There was no way I could create that truth. I also knew that I didn't want to view life from a place of illusion. I could only see it clearly if I looked at it realistically.

I felt as though I was in a race against time. So much to do, so much to accomplish, and it wasn't getting done. I'd wake up in the morning with a full agenda. I knew that all I had to do was write it down, check it off, and it would get done. But I didn't know what to do first. Confusion reigned.

I was also under the illusion that I didn't need any outside help, that I could do everything by myself. My mother told me that I'd been that way from the time I was very small. I remember having a spinning-top toy as a child. That was what I was doing: spinning, spinning, spinning. A spinning top stays where it is. When I was a little girl, my brothers and I would twirl around and around until we would fall to the ground from dizziness. I would laugh and laugh; it was great fun.

Life sometimes seemed like that. I could spin and spin until all control was gone. By control, I mean the ability to go forward without confusion. Confusion cast a cloud over me, and I couldn't think clearly. It's like I had an organized desktop with little notes of what to do and in the order of when to do them, but a wind would come along and blow all of the notes off the desk. I couldn't catch them, and the few I did weren't in order. All of my work went right out the window.

My older brother, Tom, has always been my protector. I felt safe with him and knew that no harm would come to me if he were around. When he was five and I was four, he put me into his little red wagon and told my parents, "I'm taking Mary Jean away from here because she's not treated good." He pulled me down the street away from our home, taking me to safety.

There were many times in my life when I didn't feel safe. I'm not talking about being alone on a dark road at night. I'm talking about being at a party with unfriendly, unfamiliar faces, or visiting a new city and not knowing how to navigate around it.

But I knew that if I had confidence in myself, I would be safe. I didn't have to be perfect or say just the right thing. I just had to be myself. What a novelty. But that wasn't how it always was until I came out of the illusion of trying to be perfect. Renata helped me throw away all of my veils.

Illusion and confusion don't reign anymore in my life. I'm not a prisoner. Now I'm free because of the new and different path that I took, which had little rest stops along the way. I stopped for meditation, deep breathing, acceptance, non judgement, and living in the now. Bye-bye, illusion and confusion! Hello, freedom!

"LEARN TO COME FROM THE HEART AND NOT THE MIND."

Renata would say, "Go to the heart; find the love within you. You've seen what love has done by communicating with your dad and Forrest. They've shown you great love by helping you."

I started to realize that she was right: I needed to go to my heart. But how? What a different approach. I didn't know how to start. I decided to make a conscious effort and found that I could open my heart through meditation, yoga, and Deeksha. I could change and heal by asking for the unconditional love that resided within me. The answers weren't in my mind. I could never find them there. But I'd never considered they could be in my heart. How can something so small hold such a vast amount of feelings?

I found out over time that my heart was full but always open to receiving more. That seems like a dichotomy, but it isn't. The method of measurement is different. It's not defined by earthly calculation. It has a spiritual tape measure that never runs out. It is infinite. Just when I think it's full and cannot accommodate any more, I'm fooled. More warm, loving feelings arrive and my heart embraces them.

There's a lot more to the heart than the size and the pumping of the blood. It's an open vessel with a welcome sign on it, a precious jewel that pumps both blood and love. I could see the blood. I could feel the love. All I had to do was open the my heart's door. I was constantly aware of the wonderful work it does to keep my body and spirit going. I like that feeling of an unlimited supply. I didn't have to horde it in case there was a shortage. There never was, and never will be. It grows with abundance.

I compare my heart to my car. When my gas tank gets too low and it needs more energy, I go to the station and put in some gas. Similarly, I go to my heart and fill it with love and good energy at the gas station of love. This was possible because of Renata and meditation. My heart was filled with fear, judgment, nonacceptance, and worry. Slowly, the negative emotions were replaced by trust and love.

Love beams out like a laser ray. It encompasses all those who are drawn to it. Fear repels; love is like a magnet. Going into the rays of love changed my perceptions. It's as though I realigned myself. The body realigns via physical manipulation, acupuncture, craniosacral therapy, and yoga. The mind and spirit realign through love. Fear used to seep out of me; now it's love. I opened myself to the idea that my heart was a receptacle that embraces love. Now, it's constantly full, and when I give love, more comes back. My love goes with me all the time; all I have to do is recognize that it's been in my heart forever.

My eyes need glasses to see clearly; they help with the details and the fine print, so to speak. But I haven't always seen the fine details of my spiritual life—I had to seek to find them. Looking through the glasses can give me one kind of a picture, but adding the eyes of my heart can change it completely. My eyes with glasses see the tremendous beauty of nature; my eyes of my heart look at that beauty and want to preserve it.

My eyes with glasses see people in the various modes of doing. My eyes of the heart see them in a different way. I can see their sorrow, confusion, anger, and unhappiness.

My heart opens up and fills with love for them. I don't know what has happened in their lives, but I can see the end result. I know they hurt; I know I've hurt. It's all the same. My heart knows that. It shines with love like a beacon. Sometimes the light can fill my whole being and radiate out to others who are living lives of desperation. When I leave the house, I sometimes forget my eyeglasses, but not my heart glasses.

* * *

Working in the garden has always been one of my greatest pleasures. I feel a connection to the earth when my fingers are entwined with the soil. I've spent countless hours digging, planting seeds, and transplanting flowers until they find a spot to flourish in. I've had many gardens, which have all grown with great bounty. I've fed them, watered them, and generally just taken care of them; and I've been rewarded with a glorious multicolored garden. I now sit in the midst of the garden and marvel at the splendor.

How could this be? I'd plant a seed, and in the spring a plant would break through the ground then reach up so the sun could give its warmth to it. When fall comes, the plant would go to sleep for the winter and wake up again in the spring to bring its beauty into the world. All I had to do was give the plants what they needed to grow and flourish. Maybe they didn't get the sun every day, but what was given to them the day before kept them going.

My body and heart are the same. If I treat them kindly and with love, they also flourish. I go to sleep at night and regenerate. I feed my body, exercise it, and am kind to it. I do the same for my heart. I feed it with kindness and compassion so it can open more. I see a garden of the mind. I can weed out what I don't want and grow more of what's good for me. I can plant anything at any time; I'm not concerned about the seasons. I am from the earth. I just happened to be a different variety of plant. A rose is exquisite. I'm glad I'm human, with a heart.

The washing machine rotates so the clothes can get clean. The dryer spins them dry. The toaster makes toast. The dishwasher washes dishes. The vacuum cleaner cleans. There is a purpose for every appliance. The car allows me to go short or long distances. My hands allow me to do a variety of tasks. My eyes allow me to take in information. My brain allows me to assimilate information. But my heart is the greatest organ. It fills up with love and emanates that love to others. It always has room to fill up with more love, and it affects all parts of my body. The love within it makes my aliveness joyful and peaceful. I can live without the appliances, but not my heart.

A wave of contentment sweeps over me. I've gained a gentle force, and I am humbled by that.

* * *

CHAPTER 15

PRAYERS FROM RENATA

"OUR THOUGHTS CREATE OUR REALITY"

How can reality be affected by thoughts? If my thoughts tell me someone is angry with me, then that's reality. But, as I found out, it's not, really, I only think it is. My reality changes when I find out that this person isn't angry with me. I had a lot to learn.

A star falls from the sky and disappears into the atmosphere. Thoughts and ideas seem to come in like that or like a tornado. Bam! There's a thought. Pow! Another one. Sometimes that's how it felt to me. Oneness-Deeksha believes thoughts are all around us. They are ours for the taking or rejecting. They've been here since the beginning of time.

I had different thoughts, some in the forefront and others trying to get out. I pushed down those trying to be heard and only listened to the obvious ones. I thought, If I let one out, the floodgates will open, and I'll have to listen to all of them.

There were too many powerful, unpleasant, scary and upsetting thoughts so I submerged them. I knew that many of them were connected to my feelings about my mother. I didn't know all the others, and the fears and anxieties associated with them; but I carried all that around, unaware of the weight that they created.

Renata, meditation, and Oneness-Deeksha taught me that I didn't have to accept the thoughts that came into my head. I could filter them out. I had to find that out before I could accomplish it. I gave life to problems, but they were only there to be solved. They didn't define me as a person and weren't life threatening.

I had to learn to tell the thoughts I didn't want: "Leave now!" Many times they wanted to hang around, but I insisted they leave. We did have battles, but I finally won. I remember thinking that thoughts should have little tabs on them so I could pull out the ones I wanted. In a way I can do that now. If a negative thought comes in that I don't want, I can grab the tab and throw it away. I can say, "That's not good for me. I don't want it. Don't intrude into my territory. Get out!" I can pick and choose my thoughts and am not bound to them just because they've entered my mind. I can just throw them to the wind, as thoughts are just a form of energy.

Renata told me, "You must have borders. Borders create safety, self-confidence, and respect. The borders I'm talking about are the borders of the mind. If you allow anything or everything to come in and have the same thoughts continually, then you're hostage to your emotions. To be free, you must filter what you allow in. This takes vigilance."

Today, I'm not a prisoner of my thoughts, nor am I my thoughts. I can create how I want to live. I can choose to have pleasant, loving thoughts. I can be positive. I base it on reality. I can't physically build my house, but I can change how I perceive my house. I can see lightness or darkness—it's all up to me. There's nothing hidden to deal with. I deal with what is in the now. It was hard to do at first, but I've become pretty good at picking and choosing. I choose so many other things in my life, so why not my thoughts?

I see a wall with water running down the front of it. The water joins in with the river at the bottom of the wall and continues to roll along the valley. The waters mingle and nurse the earth. I am nursed with new ideas and thoughts that enter from the outside. I can have some stay and they mingle with the thoughts I've already accepted. To be able to choose is freedom.

I can gather new information, and my thinking can change. But I can't change if I don't mingle the old with the new. I can decide what makes sense to me and what doesn't. My path is not straight and narrow; it ambles here and there. I can always learn something new along the way. I want to mingle my thoughts the way the water does. I am thirsty for that.

I learned to truly change my thinking. It's like anything else that has to be learned—a new sport, a new game. It has to be worked on every day, and then it's easier the next day. I start by saying, "That fact doesn't apply to me now," and after I've said that for a while, it becomes easier to tackle and change the next thought. The thought could be something I'd done in the past that I would do differently today. I tell myself, "Don't grab onto it; it doesn't do me any good today. It doesn't apply to me now because my thinking is different. I handle situations in a different manner."

Once I recognized that fact, I was able to reject old thought patterns. It's like playing baseball as a kid and not swinging at certain pitches due to the fear of striking out. It took time to learn. The sport of living takes time, also.

Today, I like to constantly hone my game, and I often feel like I've just hit a home run.

* * *

It was a long time before I accepted another dimension that I could access. My first experience was when I was 12 years old and going to Catholic school. The nuns thought I had the makings of becoming a nun, and they pretty much convinced me that would be my destiny.

One night I awoke from a sound sleep. It was dark outside, but my room was filled with light. I sat up in bed, looked around my room, and knew that I was awake. I looked at the mirror and saw the face of Jesus with the crown of thorns on his head. I can't explain why with mere words, but I knew, at that moment, that I would never be a nun after that experience. I'd received a message. I laid my head down and never again considered that my destiny was to be a nun.

I never discussed this with anyone until one day I was talking to Renata and told her about it. She explained that the reason I saw Jesus was because I could identify that face. Spirit came in to help me. I know now that we can get messages from spirit. My message was in the form of a realization, not words.

My late husband, Mort, was in the hospital during the last six weeks of his life. Valarie would get calls in the middle of the night and would immediately go to the hospital to help him. Forrest sat by his bedside and held his hand for hours. Mort was valiant and never talked about the fact that he was going to leave the planet.

At the end, he was in a coma for a day and a half. Valarie and I were at his bedside, and we saw him take his last breath. As I mentioned earlier in this book, we saw a white light go under his skin through his entire body, then leave and spiral from the crown of his head and go up through the ceiling of his room. We looked in amazement at each other. We both said, "Did you see that? What an experience!" That was my first confirmation of the spirit leaving the body.

With Forrest, he just left; I didn't get to see him leave. I was devastated at the time, and deluded myself on a deep level that he was on vacation. I knew rationally he wasn't, but I needed to hold that idea in some part of my brain.

I close my eyes, and his face is before me. In that sense, he isn't gone. I can almost feel him. I don't think a mother ever loses that connection. He is still my son, just in a different dimension. I look to the sky and know that he's up there somewhere. I didn't see his spirit leave, but I know he's around me because of my conversations with Renata.

"YOU ARE FILLING WITH SPIRITUAL FOOD AND GRATIFYING RENATA, THE CHEF."

Renata introduced me to the concept that energy or spirit resides inside me. It took me a long time to completely accept it. I slowly started calling on spirit to help me in troubled times and found a friend. Then I knew it was true. I used to think, I have to see it to believe it. But no longer. My vision has expanded to what I cannot physically see in this dimension—it's more a sense of believing and knowing. I can communicate on a different level. What's so strange about that? It's true that seeing is believing, but also not seeing is believing. Spirit is eternal; mine has been in different bodies in different lifetimes.

I was born with complete freedom and memories of the other side, but my memories were slowly stripped away from me as I became more entrenched in living life on this planet. Eventually I disconnected from my spirit, which is the true me, my source of freedom. I could never trust my own judgment; I had to look for reassurance, and I became critical of myself. It's as though I had a monitor on me, and it would go off all the time, letting me know that I should have acted differently.

That way of thinking was accelerated when Forrest left. I became hypercritical of myself. I felt that I should have been a different kind of mother, one who could take care of my children's needs. I always said, "I may not have been the best mother, but no one could love her children more—they could love them the same, but not more." My heart has always been full of love for my kids. They are wonderful beings full of light.

There were times when I felt I was all alone with no one to help me. Despair and panic overcame me. But I came to realize that I'm never alone. I may think I am, but that isn't true. I can call on my spirit anytime I want. It's like picking up the phone and calling a friend I really trust, with the guarantee that he or she will do whatever I need for my greater good. When I get into a bad place, I take some deep breaths and ask for help.

I created my own holy place, a little altar, where I burn a candle or incense and sit on the floor in a lotus position. I find inspiration that I never thought I would possess. And I can do all this by being alone.

Why was it so hard to learn these life lessons? I didn't know, but learning a new and better way to handle situations at times was as difficult as it must be for a baby bird to learn to fly. The bird gets his freedom, and so did I.

Today, I know that even if my newfound sense of peace is a momentary reprieve, I'm prepared for what is to come. My heart is open. I can think of my son and not break down, as he's in a special place in my heart. I love him deeply, but I don't have to say good-bye because he's waiting for me on the other side. Someday I will see him again. I'm not in a hurry to leave this planet, but what a reunion we will have when I do!

Life is exciting, challenging, painful, and beautiful. The rewards are plentiful, my psyche is free and clear, my energy is strong and constant, and my heart beams with love. It's like scratching a piece of paper that has color appear, and the more you scratch, the more colorful it becomes. That's what happened when I connected with spirit; the colors got brighter, the sounds became more pleasant, and the smells grew more fragrant. Living life is a different experience than it was before. It was hard to connect to my true spirit, but I persevered; I just kept on scratching.

Renata recommended that I do the following exercises and practices. I continue to use them, and whenever I do, I lovingly think of her.:

1. I ask St. Germain to put a violet flame around my aura and take all the negative thoughts and fears to the flame and transmit them to neutral. It works. I can call on masters from the other side to help me. They're waiting lovingly, full of compassion and pure love. I don't need a phone to call them.
2. Here's how to clear and heal your aura:

    a. Ground yourself.
    b. Close your eyes; feel the area around your body. Breathe, and extend your breath into the auric field—use intent. Get a sense of what your aura feels like.
    c. With breath and visualization, observe how far your aura extends in front, back, and to either side of your body.
    d. See and feel your aura above your head and below your feet. Compare the two areas.
    e. Imagine filling a giant egg with your aura.
    f. Observe changes in feeling, physical sensations, and awareness.
    g. Visualize a rain shower of golden liquid light pouring down on your aura. Let it rain two to five minutes. Notice how wonderful this feels.

h. Visualize a violet-colored flame the size of your aura. Put it around the entire aura. Violet flame translates lower frequency energies into a higher frequency. Do this one to two minutes. Too much will make you feel overwhelmed.
i. When complete, remove the flame and open your eyes.

CIRCLE OF PROTECTION PRAYER

Draw a circle of divine love and protection around myself.
In this circle I place:

The white light of peace,
The blue light of healing,
The clear red light of energy
And the powerful green light of prosperity

In the circle I further ask
that no one or nothing shall enter
if not for my greatest good

Amen

HUNA PRAYER

If I have hurt someone today
in thought or word or deed,
or failed another in his need
I now repent.

If I could take those steps again,
tomorrow I will make amends,
and heal with love those hurts.
I do know this request:

If someone has hurt me deep
and no amends are made,
I asked the light to balance all
I count the debt is paid.

Parental spirits whom I love
and who I know love me,
reach through the door I open wide,
make clear my path to thee.

Max Freedom Long

Renata also told me: "Sit with your feet firmly on the ground, visualize a violet light going up to the top of your legs, and breathe deeply. That will ground you." It has worked every time. It makes me feel that I am completely in touch with my body.

Renata once asked me, "If you had a religion, how would you define it?" After much thought this is what I decided:

- Be kind to everyone
- Be tolerant
- Everyone is equal
- Cherish children
- Don't judge
- Respect your fellow man, especially older people
- Be honest with everyone, including yourself
- Don't take what doesn't belong to you
- We make our own choices before we come to this planet
- We are learning lessons
- Believe in a higher soul
- Don't lie or cheat
- Our soul always was and always will be; our light shines for eternity
- Believe in reincarnation
- Buddha, Mohammed, Moses, and Jesus are of the same soul

- Meditate to find contentment and peace because then we truly can become love
- When you learn all your lessons (which are about relationships), you unite with your higher soul and become one with other souls

The circus is coming to town. The huge tents are anchored into the ground with large bolts. I became bolted into the ground through Renata. She started with little brads, progressed with small nails, then large nails, and finally the bolts. I am firmly anchored, but the amazing part is that I can roam around. I don't have to stay in one place. I never lose the anchor. The tent poles are taken out of the ground, the tents are folded, and they're moved to a new location to be bolted again. There's no stability otherwise. I can go anyplace, do anything, and my stability stays.

The acorn falls to the ground, and the squirrel scrambles to capture it. He digs a hole and buries it so he can save it for a winter snack. He forgets where it is, and a little sprig pops out of the ground in the spring. Out of that sprig will grow another oak tree. Mother Nature supports the flourishing of life on this planet. An acorn was planted for me by Renata. She made it grow until a little tree appeared. She helped me water and feed it until it blossomed full of beautiful green leaves. I can stand tall now because the burdens of the past are gone. The winds of awareness blew them away. I am grateful to live with my roots firmly planted into the ground.

* * *

CHAPTER 16

HEALING

While healing, I found out that I had to deal with many issues such as anger, the need to change, living in the moment, having choices, being connected, fear and sorrow, and being grateful. I call this "My Coming Back."

ANGER

When a hurricane hits, it uproots trees, blows off roofs, and saturates the ground with water. When my anger hit, it uprooted me and blew me away from my center, saturating my body. It completely unsettled me, creating stress and causing my muscles to tighten. As a result, I got headaches, as well as shoulder and backaches. I thought that reacting with anger, which I used to call force, was good for me, but I was constantly getting upset. My life never spun completely out of control, but it sometime seemed close. I finally asked myself, "What can I do?" I had to address the anger by recognizing it and then changing my reactions to situations.

For years I didn't know that I could actually change my reactions. A great deal was learned behavior, and then I added my own emotions; the pot was brewing all the time. I couldn't imagine that there was any other way to live. If a ball was thrown at me and it was going to hit me, my reaction would be to step aside or duck. That made sense. I finally realized that if I was angry, I could make the choice not to react. Before, this might have been quite challenging, but my awareness and perception enabled me to act differently as I moved forward on my path. I no longer wanted any hurricanes to descend on me.

I read the newspaper, read the news on the internet, and watched the news on TV. But what I really needed was good news of spirituality to balance out all of the other news, all the angry voices. I didn't want to live in anger or be fearful about what was going to happen next. I acknowledged that generally the world operates on fear, standing one's ground, not listening to the other side, and maligning others. That thinking is diametrically opposed to the way I wanted my thinking processes to be. If someone else is angry, I know that I don't have to be part of that person's drama. Drama belongs on the stage or in the movies, not in my life.

I had the choice of getting upset or taking everything in stride. Yoga teaches that bodies change chemically when anger sets in, and takes hours for them to return to normal. Why put myself through that? I decided that I could react in another way. I could accept what came along and deal with it. It took time for me to learn this. I didn't learn it in a school classroom. I learned this in the classroom of life. I don't carry around schoolbooks. I carry my toolbox, and everything I need to help me is in there. I can get an A or a C. It's up to me.

I am so much more aware now. Before, I couldn't imagine that there was any other way to live. I knew that behavior patterns have been addictive for me. Now I know that I can break the addiction. There have been different tools I've used to get to that place: meditation, yoga, talking with the other side through Renata, and Oneness Blessing/Deeksha.

BALANCE

To keep my body in good working order, I go to the doctor periodically. The same can be said about my mind. I've found that balance is the key to good mental and spiritual health. If my body is out of balance, I can get a physical ailment. If my mind is out of balance, I can get a spiritual ailment. I meditate and do yoga to balance my body and mind. The tree pose is a good one—my body balances and my mind focuses. I've also learned to slow down. I take a deep breath and get back into balance. I want my spiritual feet firmly rooted.

I don't like scary movies. They upset me. I can walk out if I want to, but I can't always walk away from disturbing episodes in life. There's another option: stay balanced. People can be confrontational and try to push my buttons. Thankfully, I disabled my buttons, and I don't add to their stress by responding back. I found out that by being calm, others become calmer. There's nothing for them to defend. I know that some people think that this is weak, but I look at it as a conscious decision. It's not a matter of being weak or strong; it's coping with life. I'm not threatened in any way, because I've found out that I'm able to make the decision to not take the bait. I know how fish are caught—by taking the bait, they die. I don't want my spirituality to die.

CHANGE

My concern about changing was: Who will I be? Will I like myself? Will people find me different and want the old me back? How will I handle change? Will my loving feelings be the same? I was familiar with the old me. I viewed changing as flipping completely upside down. There were things I wanted to change about myself, but to change completely . . . well, I didn't know if I liked that idea. I wanted a new process of thinking to enter magically—I could wave my wand and all would be different.

I believed magic happens because it did when I was little: Santa, the Easter bunny, the Tooth Fairy, and so on. My uncle did magic tricks and coins disappeared. So I believed. But now it was different, I had to deal with reality, and that was hard. I didn't think I could do it. A part of me thought my life reactions were okay. It took me a while, but I got the message. I needed to guide my own life. I had to make the changes and go where I'd never been.

I was afraid, but I was slowly able to change by weeding out old patterns of thinking, which was difficult and laborious. I went into new territory, and it welcomed me with open arms. Do I want to bring the magic back into my life? Yes, sometimes, but I know it doesn't work. To change wasn't magical. It was like keeping my eye on the ball, the first rule in tennis, and the same when changing is the goal. I had to realize I wanted to change, and then find out how to go about it. Then I had to do it! I started with small steps, recognizing what had to be done through meditation, yoga, and mostly Renata. I realized that there was no alakazam! No rabbit in the hat. I didn't need Houdini.

When Forrest left, I didn't know where I was going, I just wanted him back and wanted to survive. That's all I thought about. I carried his picture with me and kissed it all the time. My mind was full of longing. I used to think, If I could see his face only for a moment, that would help. After a long period of time, I thought about survival. Slowly I climbed that mountain of despair, reached the top, and slowly started back. I didn't have mountain-climbing tools, just utter despair. I got there by living one more day, one more day, then another, then another, until one day there was a momentary reprieve from the anguish. Slowly, more moments arrived, and I was able to see that maybe I could live without sadness and despair. As devastating as it was when Forrest left, a new path was opening up for me.

One summer while visiting Porto Ercole, Italy, I went for a morning walk and came upon a field with hundreds of small red poppies. That's all I could see as they dotted the landscape. As I was walking alone on two-lane dirt roads, it seemed like a scene from a time long ago—no cars in sight, just peace.

The previous winter had been extremely cold, and freezing weather had descended onto Italy. Many olive trees and plants, particularly bougainvillea, were injured or died. But many of them fought back. The flowers were starting to bloom on the bougainvillea. I wanted to cheer them on. "You can make it, you can make it." Encouragement and a little rah-rah helped me. I told myself when I was in the depths of despair or if the situation seemed impossible to resolve, "You can do it, you can do it." There were two choices for me: stay stuck where I was and never flower, or open the buds and tell myself, "You can do it."

It was a jumpstart for me. I can see the gnarled olive trees and the injured bougainvillea and know that they bloomed again with the nurturing of nature. I found that I could nurture myself by changing my self-perception and my ability to climb out of the depths of despair.

Everything changed. My body felt different every day—some days with more energy, some less. Some days I could accomplish more than others. Some changes were permanent. An obvious one is that my son will never come back here during my lifetime. I can't do anything about that. But I know that my life will continue to change. My only question is: How? I don't know that answer. Will it be for better or worse? I don't know that answer either. Nothing will ever be the same again. But there's no turning back; there is only moving forward.

Renata once told me, "If there's a potential problem, you have to have an intent of what to do to solve it, put into action all that you can do, and then give it up and trust. Trust in the universe that the outcome will be what is best."

So I accept that now. I remember having outcomes I didn't understand and then years later seeing the reason for them. I don't like the outcome that involved Forrest leaving, but I understand how it changed my life and started to move it in a different direction.

Now, the sun shines every day. Sometimes I can't see it because of the cloud formations, but I know that it's there. I never used to think about that. What else has been so consistent in my life? Loved ones have gone, my body has gone through changes, I've moved to different places, and I constantly meet new people. Change has been constant. But I do have the power over some changes. I can pick and choose which feelings bring about the changes I want in my life. I can choose love instead of fear. I can feel compassion for all people.

I leave myself open for new ways of thinking to enter. I look forward to seeing the magnificent sun every day and the magnificent new choices entering my life.

New beginnings and new ways of thinking . . . new thinking has absolutely brought about new beginnings for me. More joy and looking at relationships from a new perspective have come about. I know it all depends on me and my attitude. I could have a different relationship with my mother today. I do have a different relationship with my family. I've learned that I constantly change, and relationships change. It's a simple equation I never thought possible.

I see a huge field of small stones and decide to clear an area so my bare feet won't hurt when I walk. It's taken a long time to clear the site, and I've labored day by day. I directed my energy and time there. Finally, success! I can play there, I can rest there, I can have a picnic there, I can sit and read there, and I can have friends there. The area is different because I cleared out the pebbles. My life is different because I cleared out the old thinking and brought in the new.

LIVING IN THE MOMENT

I wasn't familiar with the concept of "living in the moment." I learned that the past grabbed me and the future worried me. I prevented myself from going forward because I was stuck. I didn't believe I could give up my old patterns of behavior. I had to get used to the concept and then work on adopting it.

Huge, soft snowflakes are falling onto the ground. It's the first snow of the winter. The flakes linger on the branches of the trees and gently carpet the ground. I'm happy, even if only for a moment, because peacefulness descends upon me. That feeling is fleeting at times, when I remember all that I have to do. But if I capture the picture of the moment and recall that during the day, I can be in that moment of peacefulness. There can be chaos all around me, but I can remove myself from it, maybe only for a short time, but I will be removed.

When I was a child, there was always something to explore. I remember that I could hardly wait for spring. One day the sun would be shining, the trees would be starting to bud, the violets would be blooming, and the pollywogs would be emerging. I picked a handful of violets and caught some pollywogs to put into a jar. I ran home, put the flowers into water, watched the pollywogs for a while, then released them back where I found them. The joys of life have changed over the years, but they're always there. I didn't always know that; I wasn't aware. I was in a different form of consciousness. There is a saying, "One cannot see the forest for the trees." That's where I was, but Forrest helped me get out.

Father Time marches on, and I'm willing to walk to the beat. Instead of longing for days that are gone, I live for the day that is here. I only have the moment. All previous moments have added up to my present day. I want to live my present moment to the fullest. I want to really hear conversations that are taking place. I want to see the bounties of Mother Nature clearly and with open eyes. I want to love my family and friends with depth and appreciation.

I want to hear music with my ears in the moment. I want my senses to be alive to receive all experiences with open arms.

The yellow beams of the sun touch a great old tree and illuminate its leaves to a brilliant green. It's a sight to behold. My eyes are filled with the beauty of this planet. Mother Earth has been good; she shares her bounties with everyone. Turmoil hits, and she repairs the damage. It may take some time, but the trees and flowers grow again. My life is embraced by her. She provides, no matter what the day sends—sun, rain, or snow. The air I breathe is a luxury I didn't think about often. I now appreciate what is given to me because it can be gone in a second. I drink in what is happening. The oak tree basks in the sun, and I bask in the now.

All moments accumulate into hours, hours into days, and days into years. It's like building a house brick by brick and loving it when it's done. But it's never done. I can add onto it. I can change the interior or exterior as I go along. It keeps changing, but it's the same. It gets older and increases in value, and the memories living in it enhance the value for me. It is home. It is comfort. It is a refuge. Each moment is to be cherished. I have built my life brick by brick. I change the interior or exterior periodically. I feel comfortable today, in the moment. I will continue to do that and enhance the quality of my life I sit at my window watching beautiful white butterflies flutter by as they go south for the summer. Every year it's the same journey. They know where they're going from the instant they leave their cocoon. How fortunate they are.

I didn't know for sure where I was going and when I would leave. I thought of the consistency of it all, how nice and safe. I was never sure where my path would lead me. I learned; had many good times with family and friends; and had much love, joy, and sorrow.

At times I think I would have enjoyed flitting here and there like a butterfly, but I would have missed all the wonderful times in my memory bank. Butterflies not only flutter, but take the time to sit on a flower or tree and linger there a while. They are in the moment; that's all they have. That's all I have, also, and I will cherish each moment. I will linger like a butterfly.

* * *

CHAPTER 17

WINNING

CHOICES

Choices, choices, choices. I wasn't aware of how my choices were determined by my past experiences and past lives. My emotions blinded me from making healthy ones. I like to cook and try new recipes. But what would my recipe be for living my life? Cooking dinner is like living life. There are recipes that are delicious and healthy, and some delicious and unhealthy. Which would I choose? I hoped to find some good recipes.

Relationships have always been important to me. I liken them to bread. I like some types of bread more than others, preferring whole wheat or raisin. I can like or love different people, but maybe they're not all whole wheat or raisin; maybe a part of them is rye. A little piece of rye now and then doesn't mean I can't enjoy the rest of them. Tasting the rye makes me realize how much I love the other kinds of bread. I can take the raisin with a little rye now and then if I want. It's my choice.

I see a beautiful blue sky. The color radiates and changes the perception of my life; it raises my spirits. I feel different if it's raining or cloudy. Colors have always had that effect on me. Green calms me, yellow creates sunshine, and sky blue and shades of purple are easy on my eyes. Red is fiery. People used to have that effect on me, also. A bright smile radiates and is contagious. A scowl is unpleasant. I can pick colors, choose to wear a smile, go to movies I like, and listen to music that pleases my ears. I can also choose to live my life in the way I want to. I can perceive people and their actions in a negative or positive way. A blue sky or dark cloudy one . . . it's all up to me.

Over the years I've collected seashells. Carol, my yoga teacher in Florida, went to the Turks and Caicos Islands and brought back the most beautiful and intricate piece of work from the ocean. It's like a small fan with lacy designs throughout. I marveled at the intricacy. I see life as having many intricacies, and they can all work together to create beauty and harmony. It's my choice to see life in that way.

I remember walking behind my father in the snow and putting my feet into the footprints left by his feet. That was fun—little feet stepping into the prints of larger feet and being aware of how lucky I was to be with someone whose larger feet could do things I couldn't do. Today, I know that I can walk in someone else's footprints or walk in my own. I make that choice.

To me, that's how I found the truth and ability to go on. I learned from many sources, but I had to make the final decision. I'm grateful to everyone who has touched my life. I made choices along the way that moved me in a certain direction and went only where my feet could go. I do not want to piggyback on anyone else, not even my father, whom I love so much.

I played games as a child—some I was good at, some not. My life isn't a game. I could take irresponsible chances in a childhood game, but not in my life. I was somewhat of a daredevil while I was young, but after growing up, I realized that this wasn't prudent. I believed in taking chances, but just with more safety attached. Now I believe that choice is the route for me. I can choose every day to make little decisions or big decisions. I am now a choice taker, not a chance taker. The daredevil is gone. That path no longer serves my purpose.

Apples are entirely different from oranges. I can't compare them. I don't like the taste of one more than the other. Sometimes I like apples and sometimes oranges, but I always prefer one over the other. That pertains to all choices for me. It doesn't mean I can't see the value of what I don't choose. The important element to me is . . . I can choose. Differences aren't important.

One, two, three, four . . . which will I pick? I will pick what is good for me. My path is chosen by me. No matter what happens, I can choose to go wherever I want. It may take a while to decide, but I can decide. This is one of the most wonderful lessons I've learned on this journey. It's up to me. I can choose what is healthy. I can plan a trip, decide where I want to go, and how to get there. I can fly, take the bus, take the train, or drive. I can take the scenic route that might take longer, or a not-so-interesting, faster route and get there quicker. It's all my choice. I can meditate or not meditate, that's my choice.

I can be positive or negative—that's my choice. I can change how I view life—that's my choice. I can view people from a different perspective—that's my choice. I can make life easier or harder. My life changed when I fully realized that all choices are mine.

Nelson Mandela is a perfect example of choosing. He suffered for years, imprisoned in a small cell, but when he was freed, he had compassion for those who incarcerated him. What a remarkable man. He forgave. He chose to take that road. Similarly, I know I can choose whatever road I want to.

COMPARING AND WINNING

The magnolia tree is beautiful, with shiny green leaves and white fragrant flowers sitting on its branches in their full glory. People stop, stare, and drink in its beauty. They wait every year for the blooms to arrive. Finally, they do. The crepe myrtle bursts forth with its beautiful pink flowers. They know they're beautiful, and people do, too. I see these two different, magnificent specimens and enjoy the individual beauty of each. I don't compare them and say that one is more spectacular than the other.

I like to look at people in that way, too. Each one has his or her own beauty. There doesn't have to be a number one. Everyone can be number one in different ways. I believe that being human connects us on the outside and the inside. We are wonderfully and beautifully different, to be enjoyed. Just like the magnolia and the crepe myrtle trees.

I accept our differences. I can cook better than you can. I can play tennis better than you can. I jog every day and you don't. I have a bigger house than you do. My car is more expensive than yours. My child is smarter than yours. I make more money than you do. Compare, compare. That's a big part of our upbringing and adult life. But that kind of thinking can separate me from others. If I'm looking at our differences and comparing, then there's a division between us.

I am different from my family members, but alike. I have four brothers; that's an obvious difference. But we are alike in our thinking sometimes. If others have more and supposedly better things than I have, it doesn't mean anything. It doesn't make them better than I am. It only means they have more stuff.

As a kid I played marbles with my brothers. We kept the marbles in large glass jars and viewed them daily as though they were precious gems. We counted them every night to see who had the most. The winner had a sense of pride because he or she had the most. There were some marbles more aesthetically beautiful than others, so that entered into the equation as to who had the best collection. Quantity opposed to quality—which was better? We finally agreed that quantity won out.

At one time, I seemed to measure the quality of my life and who I was by the amount of material possessions I had. The more I had, the better I felt about myself. I now know that this is a false sense of security.

The most important possessions in my life are my loved ones and an abundance of compassion, connectedness, and respect for my fellow man. That is true quality and security. The security lies within myself, and it never goes away. Material possessions can come and go, but that doesn't affect how I feel about myself. I have beautiful jars of marbles all around me.

Competitiveness used to be a big part of my life. I was raised to win. Members of my family were measured by our accomplishments. That's how I measured my self-worth. If I won, I felt good about myself. That led me to want to win more and more, which could also lead to hurting people. At times I've been hurt, and I suppose I've hurt others. Because of what I've learned, I'm no longer competitive. I had to recognize the problem and then work to increase my self-esteem. I did that by coming to terms with my life and accepting who I am. It took many hours talking with Renata and meditating to decipher the puzzle.

BEING CONNECTED

I think differently than you do. I act differently than you do. I now find that makes life interesting. My four brothers and I think alike sometimes, but many times we do not. There's a common thread that runs between us, a familiarity and connection because of being children from the same family.

I've heard people in other families say, "Jane is exactly like her mother, or John is exactly like his father." I've seen similar traits between parents and children, but Jane and John's individuality is taken away when they're viewed as clones. Each of us is an individual, but connected. There are similarities among cultures, but they're not all the same. They are individual. I love the individuality of the connectedness.

* * *

Gerry and I were traveling from Paris to Germany to visit a friend of ours. I had modeled with her, and we had remained friends over the years. She was also an old friend of Gerry's; in fact, she introduced us. Gerry and I were transferring from one train to the other in Germany with four minutes to get our bags from one to the other. The train we were to transfer to was on the track to the right of the train, but we'd taken our bags off to the left. We realized our mistake, grabbed our bags from the platform, and started to run through the open door of the train to the other side. I was following Gerry when all of a sudden I fell down to my waist through the opening between the train and the platform. My legs were dangling near the tracks. I was stunned and didn't know what was happening. I was in a daze and couldn't call out to Gerry. In an instant out of nowhere, I felt helpful hands under my arms that pulled me up onto the platform, but frankly, I wouldn't recognize the kind gentleman who rescued me if I saw him today.

Gerry heard the commotion, turned around, and ran over to me. After thanking the man, both he and Gerry grabbed my bags, and the man took us to our train. "Thank you, thank you. You saved my life!" I exclaimed. My heart was full of gratitude. I was very shaken because I knew what could have happened if that man hadn't helped me. We boarded and continued on our journey.

After settling down in our seats, I said, "Gerry, I don't think there was any damage. My pants got torn, but that's all." I was grateful for the outcome. But after about five minutes, my knee felt funny. I felt it and discovered a swelling the size of a grapefruit above the kneecap. Gerry called the conductor, who checked my knee. He immediately asked via the public-address system: "Is there a doctor on the train?"

A doctor responded, she checked my leg, and said, "Get off at the next stop. I will arrange for an ambulance to meet you and take you to the hospital." The train stopped, the ambulance met us, and I was put on a stretcher. We sped through the streets of Germany, arrived at the hospital, and were greeted by two doctors who checked my leg. I was getting very concerned. Gerry speaks German, so he discussed what was happening with the doctors. They said, "Your wife has a blood clot, and we will give her pain medicine, but she must see a doctor when she arrives at her destination."

Gerry called our friends, Jutte and Stephan, and explained what had happened. They were expecting us to arrive at a train station near their home in a few hours. They immediately jumped into their car and drove a long distance on a rainy, cloudy night to get us. They had blankets and pillows for me to rest my legs on during the ride to their home in the Moors.

We arrived late in the night, but the bed was ready for me, and I was gently helped into it. Our friend is a kind, capable, beautiful woman, so I was in the best of hands. The following morning she called two of her doctor friends who were retired, and they came to see me. One walked in with his black bag in hand and said, "I'm so excited to see a patient again." I laughed and felt very comfortable. Both of them examined me and came up with the same diagnosis: I was told that I couldn't take a bath or shower for days and had to elevate my leg.

Jutte also wanted me to see her doctor who had operated on her foot. He gave me a drug that I had to inject into my stomach every day to thin my blood. He told me I could fly home, and gave me medicine for the flight. I was beginning to feel like a princess because of the attention showered on me. We had a delightful visit. I couldn't do what we'd planned to do, such as walk the Moors and the surrounding villages, but my friends adjusted their schedules in consideration of me. They didn't want me to feel bad that I'd changed their plans so drastically. I was able to meet their wonderful friends, and our hostess could not have been more gracious. She constantly waited on me. I will never forget her generosity.

We flew back to Michigan, I saw my doctor, and he told me I was extremely lucky because the clot was in the muscle. I didn't tear the muscle or break anything, so I didn't need surgery.

To me, this was a perfect example of man helping man, our connectedness in full swing. I realize now that this is the flow of life, helping one another and being considerate in all ways. If someone is in pain mentally or physically, then I want to extend my hand. It has been done for me; I've been the recipient. That's how it works. Sometimes I am helped, and sometimes I help. What a perfect arrangement. We all benefit. Thank you, Jutte.

* * *

I've always loved the moon and its beauty. I often, say goodnight to the moon and Mother Earth. I feel a connection and realize that we are all kindred souls. I didn't think of those things before Forrest left. Tears fall from my eyes like lovely, soft raindrops from the sky. These are tears of joy.

CHAPTER 18

FINDING MY VOICE

FEAR AND SORROW

The last time Forrest saw his father, he told him, "I need my freedom. You understand that, don't you?" I didn't understand that statement at the time, but now I know what he meant. He was riddled with fear: fear about the future, fear about existing in the world after he got off drugs, fear that the drugs had taken his creativity away, and fear that he couldn't continue to live in such a hostile world. He mentioned his fear in his suicide letter, and he'd often told me he was shackled with fear. Fear has strength, and it won! To help my son, I would have battled those fears with the mightiest sword, but only he could overcome them.

Fear and sorrow were the only two feelings that entered my being: fear of the future without Forrest, and sorrow as I wondered how I could go on without him. I was like a walking zombie after he passed. I leaned on Gerry and Valarie as much as possible, but I've never experienced such darkness.

When the shades were drawn and the lights didn't enter anymore, life took a turn—and not for the better. Familiar feelings disappeared. Unknown, frightening thoughts replaced them. Joy and happiness were gone. I couldn't greet the day with energy or purpose; I could only view it as getting by. When and how would the shades be lifted? It felt like an impossible task. I didn't even want to try. Nothing mattered; I was confused and terrified.

However, I realized that I had to take steps to emerge from the darkness; I just didn't know how to do it. I was stuck, but I knew I had an abundance of fears to overcome: fear of being myself, fear nobody would like me when they found out who I really was, fear that Valarie would leave me, too. If one child had, why not the other? Facing those fears and others was daunting. When I realized that fear was controlling my life, I started talking to Renata, which helped lift me from the shadows and allowed me to come to terms with my misconceptions.

I also listened to Anette Carlstrom's phone calls. She explained how to connect with our Divine or Higher Intelligence, which resides inside of us, by acknowledging it. I do that while I'm meditating. I say:

> "Please help me. I need your help. You have lived within me always . . . please come forth. I love you. Please help me in my day-to-day existence. You are full of unconditional love. I thank you for all that you have done. You are my best friend. I am not afraid anymore. We travel together. Life is so much easier now. Your help has freed me. I now trust. Worry and fear have flown away. If I feel those emotions trying

> to land again, I will call on you and remind myself to trust again in the present and the future. You were there all the time, and I didn't even know it. All I had to do was find out and then ask. You are like a warm blanket . . . a special oasis. All I have to do is let your love flow through me. Thank you."

I now know that fear creates fear. I was like a mother bird flying around a baby bird who was trying to learn to fly. Only I was the baby bird. I did learn, and I can soar at times.

FINDING MY VOICE

I remember being chosen for the lead role in a school play when I was in third grade. I was excited beyond belief. My mother bought me a pink-and-maroon taffeta dress with puffy sleeves, a little collar, a full skirt, and a large wide sash at the waist. It was beautiful. I memorized my lines with glee.

Sister Suzanne was helping with rehearsals. I stood up to say my lines, but she couldn't hear me. She said, "You have to speak up, Mary Jean."

I tried to talk louder and said to myself, "Talk louder, talk louder," but I couldn't find my voice.

She said again, "Mary Jean, you have to speak louder," but I couldn't force my voice.

Finally, and with firmness, Sister said, "If you don't speak up, then we will have to replace you."

I tried and I tried, but I couldn't even hear my own voice. I was heartbroken. My voice couldn't be heard—even by me—and I lost the part. I was devastated.

I never did tell my mother because I was embarrassed, and selfishly wanted to keep the dress. I implored my brothers, Tom and Jack, "Please don't tell Mom." They agreed.

We went to school the day of the play knowing what we were doing and sat on the front steps until the play was over. We walked home, went into the house, and made believe that I'd performed. My brothers and I were sitting on the porch when a teenage neighbor who'd seen the play came to the house to see my mother.

I said, "Joanne, please, please, don't tell my mother that I lied to her." She ignored me and immediately told my mom. I got into a lot of trouble. What I'd done wasn't right, but it seemed like the only thing I could do at that time. I was afraid to tell my mother that I'd lost my part in the play.

That was not the first time I experienced an inability to speak up. It happened many times. I was worried that I might say something wrong, and I couldn't take the chance. There always seemed to be a level of terror bubbling below the surface. As time went on, I learned how to hide all of those feelings, but they were still there. No one knew but me; my secret was safe. The problem was that my body and mind knew—my stomach, in particular. It was called a nervous stomach. I was painfully thin as a child and was given horrible-tasting tonics to build me up. No one knew why I couldn't eat, and neither did I.

I knew that I didn't want to be mired in thoughts and actions from the past. I couldn't go back to my old ways of being; I had to find my voice. It had been trapped inside of me for years. I found the key and tried to unlock the chest it was confined in. It took a lot of convincing for me to allow this to happen, as I had been trained otherwise: Be nice, don't talk back, hide who you are because if you reveal that, no one will want anything to do with you. I was afraid to be the real me, to be authentic. The most amazing thing of all is that no one knew, even me for a long time. I thought that's how it had to be. But through talking with Dad, Forrest, and Renata, I finally found myself; and out came my voice.

I feel comfortable in my own skin now. I am never mean when I speak, but I am honest. The truth reigns. I could put a crown on it, I honor it so. I try to live with truth and compassion, which are two very valuable commodities. They're my gold, silver, and platinum all in one.

These precious items will never go down in value, but will only increase . . . and I don't have to worry about fluctuations. These are the precious metals in my life. I don't have to barter with anyone. They're part of my fiber.

What a wonderful journey. I've always wanted to sing, but I don't have a good singing voice. I was hoping that would change after I found my voice, but no such luck. That's okay. To have an authentic voice is more than I could have ever dreamed of. Now, maybe, I deserve to wear that taffeta dress. Just a thought.

ENERGY

Energy is everywhere, all around me.. It zigzags to the ground during a rainstorm or before a storm. I turn on the lights, the computer, the radio, the TV, and there is an instant connection. There are grids all over our country. There are radio and WiFi waves all around me. I was constantly being bombarded, and I didn't even know it. I couldn't feel them.

My emotions came in like electric waves. It was a revelation to me that I could act on every one or I don't have to if it's not right for me. I thought I was bound by whatever came into my being. Here comes another emotion . . . I like that one. I'll consider it. It was a conscious effort on my part to be aware of what was coming in. I just took for granted that I was obligated to react to the emotion of the moment.

Working with my "A Team"—Renata, Forrest, and Dad—enabled me to sort out my emotions. Now I'm relaxed about it, and amazingly, more of the emotions that are good for me arrive. I'm not being zapped anymore. I've set up my own grid. As I've said before, it's true that seeing is believing, but also not seeing is believing.

A gust of wind arises with a blast. The fronds of the palm tree fly through the air and fall to the ground with a thud. The weather goes from calm to turmoil in an instance. That happened in my life, also. There was calm, and then the phone rang. My heart crashed to the floor with a thud. My life changed—not for an instant or an hour—but forever. The frond couldn't just be picked up and disposed of, and my heart couldn't either.

I knew after a while my life would change, but little did I know how much. I've lived with the belief, "Out of something bad can come something good." I never imagined that would apply to Forrest leaving, but it does. It pains me, but it's the truth. For a time, a whole part of my life was erased. But in reality, it wasn't. He will never be gone. I never have to say good-bye. He lives in my heart. The frond didn't disappear; it was just transformed. The energy lives on.

* * *

Jackson, our cat, shimmies under a blanket and thinks he's hidden. He will peek out and look at the world with one eye and then bury his head again. He has great fun playing this game. After Forrest left, I could only peek out at the world with one eye and then go hide. The world was too blinding for me to open both of my eyes. It was as though lights would sear them, never allowing me to see again. I edged out little by little until finally I could stand up.

I see light! I see light! There's a crack under the door, and the light comes through. I want to grab it and hold it in my hand, but I can't. It's elusive. It jumps around like when I hold the mirror and direct it at the sun. But I know for sure that this is the beginning. The light may leave for periods, but it will come back, and for longer times. I breathe a huge sigh of relief. The storm is abating, and the darkness is starting to lift.

The agony is dissipating. The sun is beginning to shine again, and it warms my heart and soul. It's easier to get out of bed when morning comes. I'm not trudging with heavy feet, and I'm beginning to walk with lightness. I didn't think this day would ever come. I am surviving.

It's all the more profound because of where I've been. The contrast is sharp. Forrest's light now shines from the other side, and Valarie's does on this side. My son now has complete freedom and is astonishingly happy. And I am finally attaining freedom: freedom from what people think, freedom to go down my own path, and freedom to embrace my own thoughts.

I've found out that simple pleasures in life are truly the best. Just going along and living in the moment brings me happiness. The drama is gone. Playing with Jackson can be more fun than anything else. And going to the movies with Gerry is number one. Talking on the phone with my family and friends is also an incredible pleasure. I'd always heard the phrase "Stop and smell the roses," and now I know exactly what that means. I have a bouquet near me at all times.

I lived in a compartmentalized way: one section with anger, one section for fear, one section for bravado, one section for survival, one section for mistrust, one section longing for acceptance, and one section for worry. My challenge was to learn how to figure out what was healthy and what to throw away.

It was doubly hard not really knowing that there were sections. I actually thought I was whole. I looked whole—no one could see lines on my skin delineating the different parts. I walked around hiding all of the different parts until I finally decided I wanted to be whole and complete. But sorting it all out wasn't so easy. It was a long, slow, arduous process—sometimes just creeping along, and sometimes picking up speed. But I was learning, learning all along the way.

Sometimes I was afraid that if I chipped away one piece, there wouldn't be anything to fill that hole. But I chipped and chipped away until finally all of the holes were filled with love and acceptance—both of myself and others. When I look at myself now, I appear the same, but I'm not. My innermost self has healed and changed, which is definitely evident to me . . . and probably to others, too.

CHAPTER 19

GOING FORWARD

I'm sitting in my chair, pondering where I've been and where I am now.

Before, I was in a maze and couldn't get out. I thought, Maybe if I take this way I will succeed. Oh no! That didn't work. Maybe, this way will work. No, again. I was stuck for years doing the same thing, walking the same path, but I couldn't change it.

When I was young, there were no self-help books. I would go to the library in the hopes of finding something that would help me. But all I could find were academic books about psychiatry. It didn't seem as if there were any answers.

There didn't seem to be any answers after Forrest left, either. My broken heart and damaged soul needed healing, but the kind of healer I needed wasn't an M.D., osteopath, or chiropractor. The amazing discovery I made was that I had to find the healer within me, and then anything was possible.

Of course, I was guided and helped by Renata, Forrest, and my dad, but I had to find it within myself to do so. I want to make it abundantly clear that I couldn't have done any of this without them. They opened the door, just a little at a time at first, and then they would open it more and more until I knew I could handle it.

There are two mottos I lived by: "You can do it" and "When there's life, there's hope." However, after Forrest left, I discarded both of them. He couldn't do it, and there was no life. As I went down the path of recovery, I realized I had nothing to replace them with. I tiptoed for months, unable to go in any direction. It was as though my path was covered with a dense, sharp-edged shrub—saw palmetto—which is indigenous to Florida. But I didn't have a tool to cut through it. I would only injure myself more if I tried to continue on the same path.

Long, sorrowful days and nights descended upon me. I had nowhere to go to escape. I had to clear out old memories and thought patterns that were hindering my growth, and I had to begin to accept the fact that my son had left. I never imagined the changes that would take place in my life—I even moved to a different city.

Now, I feel that I was born with an empty book that only had a front and back cover. I fill in the chapters as I go along.

I had no idea that when my son left I would pack my bags, and along the way, get rid of some of the contents and put in new ones. In many ways the mystery has been solved: Why did I act and react the way I did? What could make my life happier and peaceful? How could I reach the fountain that bubbles out knowledge and love? Can I face the day with confidence so I could get through it without carrying the heavy bag of sorrow and regret? Would the burden cause me to fall down and never get up?

I didn't know the answers to any of these questions. I just knew I had to do something different so the light could shine again. In the end, I realized how lucky I was to have Forrest as long as I did. His face hasn't gotten any dimmer over time. I can see him as clearly as I did before he left. Of course I still grieve at times. He was such a bright light.

Every year on Forrest's birthday, strong feelings come through. I remember him tenderly and go through more grieving. It's only natural, and I honor it. His birthday is a hard day for me. So many memories flood back.

I heard that it's a good idea to write in a journal, as it's helpful to jot down one's thoughts and feelings. I found out that it was true. I found clarity when I put my words down on paper. It was like solving a puzzle. The pieces came together.

I think in the way I do today because of what happened yesterday. How clear that is to me now. I'd like to say that I know the exact time and date when I had my epiphany, but I can't. I experienced small revelations at different points over the past several years. Each one created more clarity for me. A band didn't play, nor did a loud gong ring. My recognition came in the form of the realization that I was thinking differently—with more understanding and love from the heart. Life just became easier each day. I call it a raising of consciousness, or putting on glasses that magnified the important things in life and diminished old thinking patterns.

Today, it has become so natural that at times I can be lulled into thinking I was always this way. Then I recognize how much I've changed.

I didn't believe or understand when I started this journey that I could take baby steps, and then grow with confidence. But once the door was opened and I went through it, I could never go back—another ray of sunshine would come through. I remember seeing the darkness that enveloped me after Forrest left. That darkness is now gone. I am living proof that time heals all wounds. What I mean by that is that the wound is healed and a scar is visible, but the original injury doesn't give me the same type of pain—it's a memory more than a palpable feeling.

* * *

As a child, I used to get butterflies in my stomach, but not anymore. Sometimes I miss that. They're part of the lost kingdom of childhood. There are still childlike times, such as getting an ice cream cone, sitting and looking at the stars, watching the moon come up, and being transfixed by fireworks on the Fourth of July. Now I find such pleasure in the simple wonders of life.

I recall being a little girl on a swing with the cord hanging over a thick branch of a gigantic tree. My dad is pushing me. My stomach is full of butterflies. I love the feel of the wind as I swing up and up, my hair blowing back from my head like I'm in a wind tunnel. I'm flying above the ground. I'm grasping the cord and feeling very safe because my father is down on the ground. I used to love those moments. I can still recall the delight of flying high in the swing. That's good, that's very good. I can mix the old with the new. It's a great recipe for me.

My dad gave me the teddy bear that he got as a child in the early 1900s. Teddy bears are wonderful toys. They emanate comfort and security. Dad gave it to me one day and said, "Mary Jean, I have something I want to give to you." and he presented me with his own teddy bear. None of us knew he had one. I cherish that little animal, with his paws chewed on by my dad. I can almost see my father as a little boy with Teddy in his arms and the comfort he received from him. It's hard for me to imagine my parents as little children. I would think, how could they be little going through the turbulence of growing up? I viewed them as always being in charge. They weren't, but the image remains.

I can feel the different stages of life I've gone through. How different I am today from the way I was years ago.

I didn't view my parents as changing, but of course they did. They weren't always parents, but that's what they were to me. Even when I see pictures of them in their childhood, my eyes only see parents. They were multifaceted people, but I only saw them from one dimension. I limited my connection that way, but I should have viewed them in their entirety. Dad's teddy bear reminds me of that.

Because of my belief in reincarnation, I knew I had lessons to learn. I will never have to deal with them again. My relationships are deeper and more meaningful because I can trust now. I never could trust before. It's interesting to me how I eternally wanted love from my mother and couldn't get it. But I kept trying. Not loving my daughter Valarie would create a huge hole in my life that I couldn't fill. I would be hurting both of us. It's inconceivable to me that I couldn't love Valarie with my whole heart and soul. Renata said, "When we come in, we bring in genetic memories and traits. You broke the genetic chain." I do feel like I took a pair of clippers and cut them.

The cherry trees are sated with thick, white, fluffy blossoms in full bloom. They smile for all to see their beauty and splendor. Each spring this ritual happens. Our eyes are treated with a welcome gift. The scent fills our nostrils with a heavenly fragrance.

I've been filled with the beauty and grace that life has offered to me. My journey has taken me through fields of sharp stones, angry storms, crackling lightning, and tornadoes; as well as days filled with beautiful hikes over hills of green grass, trees blossoming in the spring, and meadows of lovely flowers. I'm grateful that I've gone on this journey. All the cherry trees except one are in full splendor. I can see the one bare tree, but I can revel in the beauty of the others.

I learned that I couldn't have done this all by myself. Every day when I meditate, I call upon and thank my Divine Intelligence—a loving, all-accepting, nonjudgmental force—who resides within me. There will always be a link missing, but it no longer causes a break in the chain. It has been repaired even though I can still see where the break occurred—that will never change. But what I know is that the new chain was even stronger than the old one.

Dawn breaks and a new day starts. I can wipe the slate clean each day. My insights can be different, fresh and new. When I was little, I grew physically. I got taller; my facial and body features changed. As I got older, major emotional changes occurred. The day unfolds, the sun says hello, the birds awaken and flutter their wings on their way to gather food or continue their journey. Lights are turned on in homes everywhere. People eat their favorite breakfast. The day is beginning. I have confidence that my life will continue on this path of serenity.

I don't want to go it alone. I believe that even in death we are not alone. We leave our earthly friends and family; but because of the emotional and spiritual connection to the other side, we immediately reunite with our spiritual friends and family. The light of connectedness and love makes my journey a day-by-day delight. The light dims sometimes, but it clearly lights my way.

My path seems to sparkle. I see it glistening with beautiful stars twinkling and beckoning for me to walk along it. That's how I see the rest of my life: a starlit path that will guide me to continued fullness and happiness. I'll put my dancing shoes on and frolic with the stars.

It's as though I've come home. I am settled right where I want to be. I've been to many beautiful, exciting places in my life; and some related to tragedy, but this is where I want to be. There is no longing in my soul and heart to be anyplace else. My family and friends are the garden I want to be in the middle of. They fill my life with joy. Love flows from the fountain of life and infuses every cell of my body. I am singing, although no one can hear me. There is a buoyancy to my body, because contentment and peace fills it. I am safe here. It's my Shangri-La home—what a wonderful concept. It doesn't have to be a structure of physical brick, wood, or stone . . . it's a spiritual structure of love. My heart beams forth and touches other hearts. Love is the common denominator. It is as it should be.

I give thanks for all my gifts and for having Forrest in my life. There's a cord of life that connects us. I can visualize it going up into the sky, out into the universe, and connecting with him. Our loving bond is always there. There is more than my naked eye can see. He never ages because I can only see him as he was on Earth. The spirit never ages; it's eternal. My physical body will deteriorate, but not my spiritual one. My spirit grows throughout centuries, never aging, only getting wiser.

The trip has been difficult, exasperating, and frustrating; but also filled with compassion, caring, love, and peace. My spirit is there to help me. I just didn't always know that.

I believe that there is a reason for everything, and everything happens for a reason. I didn't grow up believing this. I quietly scoffed when people professed that they thought that to be true. But my thinking has changed. When a problem or a situation arose, I used to say, "I'll be glad to learn the lesson, but please just tell me what it is." Of course, I never got an answer because that's not the way it works. We're here on this path to find out the answers for ourselves.

I know now the lesson to be learned about Forrest leaving this planet. He is my teacher. He taught me while he was here, and he continues to teach me from the other side. I would not be where I am today if he hadn't left. He shows me the way.

I can physically travel to get from one place to another, and it can take hours or days. The journey can be arduous or pleasant. My spiritual journey took days in some areas, and weeks or years in others. Some of it was difficult, and some of it relatively easy. There were pleasant moments and excruciatingly painful times. I can never, and don't want to, go back to where I started. I've learned a great deal about myself. I take full responsibility for how I've handled my life. Looking back, there were situations I would have handled differently, but I can't change the past. The only choice I have is to move forward and live in the moment.

I fully realize that I couldn't have changed my perspective of life until I changed on a personal level. By that,

I mean change how I viewed my early childhood years. The influence of what I experienced in those early years was like a heavy cement block that I was carrying. I had to chip away at the block little by little until I could free myself completely.

Every morning I do my gratitude check. I'm even grateful for the sorrows I've had, as I've learned from them. I don't dwell on the past; I stay in the moment. I have a wonderful husband, who is always there for me; a loving and kind daughter; and stepsons (really, sons) who have always shown me their love. My brothers and their wives are supporting and loving. My friends have always been there, too. All of these individuals have enhanced my life tremendously. The thread that runs through all of these relationships is love—a genuine love that is never taken for granted.

Light fills my days now. I can truly say that I am healed. There is a vacancy where Forrest was, but I accept that. If I could push a button and he would be here, I would be ecstatic. But then I remember the pain he was in, and I know I wouldn't push that button. He will always be my son. I'm grateful that I had him for the years I did, and I wouldn't give up that experience, even knowing the pain that resulted from it.

I know that I can now find peace in the midst of turmoil. My journey has done that for me. If there was a bus with a sign "Destination Peace," I know that many people would board it. I would have. Now, I don't need it. I know where to find it. I don't have to take a ride or walk along the beach. It's within me. What a treasure this is. It's a privilege to wake up in the morning and be ready to face the day with happiness.

When I lay my head down, close my eyes, and take my last breath, I want to be content with how I lived my life. I believe I will have that experience now that I've taken a different path. It's not as though I was on a bad path . . . it just had more turbulence, worry, and low self-esteem.

This path I'm on now is healthy, enlightening, compassionate, nonjudgmental, and accepting of myself and others. Forrest's leaving taught me new ways to live. It challenged my thinking and propelled me to approach life in a new direction. For that I will always be grateful.

* * *

AFTERWORD

I hope that what I've written about my journey and how I got from where I was to where I am now is helpful to you if you're going through a tragedy or a difficult time. I would like to think that in some small way I've helped you find your way into the sunshine. The sun is there to shine on all of us. It doesn't pick just a few and say, "This is only for you."

My journey began with being gifted with two bipolar children. Little did I know how much their journey was tied into mine. We lived together and learned together.

I was fortunate that I found healers who helped me, such as Renata, Dr. John Upledger, and Dr. George Goodheart. I now believe that we are destined to meet certain people along the way for a reason. Some we just pass for a moment, and others for lifetimes. My husband, Gerry, has stood by my side as I've made this journey. We were destined to meet. The journey will continue. . . .

* * *

REFERENCES

DR. George Goodheart, DC

Dr. Goodheart was a revolutionary. Early in his career, he discovered the relationship between muscle function and health. Through this discovery he developed a unique testing method, eventually referred to as Applied Kinesiology (AK). Progressive chiropractors quickly recognized the groundbreaking nature of Goodheart's work, and established the International College of Applied Kinesiology. He helped people from all walks of life. He was the first chiropractor to serve the U.S. Olympic Team at the 1980 games in Lake Placid. He was featured in TIME magazine in an article entitled, Alternative Medicine Innovators, A New Breed of Healers. There are thousands of applied kinesiologists worldwide who now practice his techniques. Dr. Goodheart passed away March 5, 2008 at the age of 89.

Dr. John Upledger, DO

Dr. John Upledger, an osteopathic physician and surgeon, pioneered and developed CranioSacral Therapy following extensive scientific studies from 1975 to 1983 at Michigan State University, where he served as a clinical researcher and Professor of Biomechanics. Throughout his career as an osteopathic physician, Dr. Upledger was recognized as an innovator and leading proponent in the investigation of new therapies. His development of CranioSacral Therapy in particular has earned him international acclaim. He was named one of TIME magazine's innovators to watch in the new millennium. TIME wrote, "His treatment addresses an astonishing range of ailments by using gentle manipulation to restore normal circulation in the cerebrospinal fluid that bathes and nourishes the brain and spinal cord." He, also, is a renown author having written 8 books on CranioSacral Therapy. Dr. Upledger's CST is now taught worldwide to healthcare professionals. Dr. U[pledger passed away in 2012. leaving a legacy of over 100,000 practitioners in more than 100 countries.

Anette Carlstrom

Anette Carlstrom is a modern day Mystic, a fully Awakened Being and internationally recognized for spreading the phenomenon of Oneness Blessing. She shares her experiences of how living in peace and joy can be a natural state of being, and can be transferred to others. She can show how you can go into a deeper state of consciousness. and discover your inner presence. Anette Carlstrom is sometimes referred to as the Dali Lama of Sweden.

Dr. Deepak Chopra, MD

Dr. Deepak Chopra is a world-renowned authority in the field of mind-body healing, a best selling author and the founder of the Chopra Center for Wellbeing. A global force in the field of human empowerment, Dr. Chopra is the prolific author of more that 55 books, including 14 bestsellers on mind-body health, quantum mechanics, spirituality and peace.

Renata Moore

Renata Moore graduated from Purdue University with a degree in Psychology. She lived with and counseled bi-polar woman while attending the University studying for her Masters Degree. Renata referred to herself as an intuitive counselor and had an uncanny ability to connect with the other side. Her clients lived all around the world and she was completely devoted to them. She was due to receive a kidney while on dialysis when she passed away July 30, 2010

Chakras

Everyone has seven energy centers in their body called chakras, in which energy flows through. They are located in front of the spine and connect our psychic and physical energy systems. The state of each chakra reflects the health of a particular area of your body. If any of them are blocked our body cannot function properly and can lead to a variety of problems. Each one has a different location and color.

Root Chakra...at the base of the spine, color red

Sacral Chakra...in the lower abdomen, 2 inches below the navel, orange

Solar Plexus Chakra...upper abdomen in stomach area, yellow

Heart Chakra...center of the chest just above the heart, green

Throat Chakra...the throat, blue

Third Eye Chakra...between the eyes, indigo

Crown Chakra.. the very top of the head, violet

MIRA - Mental Illness Research Association

MIRA is a non-profit organization. Their mission is two-fold: to supply desperately needed funds for brain research and 2) to provide educational programs that can make a significant difference in the quality of life for those who are afflicted with brain diseases. It is through education that we hope to erase the stigma of mental illness that blocks proper diagnosis and treatment for millions of Americans each year.

MIRA
30200 Telegraph Rd., Suite 137
Bingham farms, MI 48025
1-248-335-0000 ext. 224

NAMI: National Alliance on Mental Illness

NAMI will find support groups and connect online in NAMI's discussion groups.

DANA.ORG

DANA is a site for current information on brain research WWW.DANA.ORG

THE AMERICAN ASSOCIATION OF SUICIDOLOGY

provides referrals to local self-help groups for survivors of suicide

WWW.SUICIDOLOGY.ORG

One can call a hospital in their area to find a support group for suicide or any loss of a loved one.

ABOUT THE AUTHOR

Mary Jean Teachman was born in Detroit, Michigan to Isabelle and George Dresbach. She went to the University of Detroit where she studied pre-law and mathematics. She married and had two children, Arthur Forrest Tull,II and Valarie Tull. She later divorced, was single for 4 years, married Mort D. Lieberman and was then widowed after 18 years of marriage. She found love again with Dr. Gerard W. Teachman and has been married for 23 years. She had a successful career for eight years as a runway and print model and appeared in Vogue magazine.

A longtime activist, she started and ran a successful campaign-RABAC... "Real Americans Buy American Cars" in the late 70's. She started the grass roots movement because the American auto industry was in a severe slump. Her idea was to help convince the American public to support the American car companies in their struggle against foreign imports and to save jobs. She distributed bumper stickers and gave interviews to the print and broadcast media.

At one point, a representative from the Japanese government came to interview her because they felt threatened by this movement. Gradually the unions adopted the project, which developed into their "Buy American" campaign

She was President of Groesback Investments for ten years and President of MIRA (Mental Illness Research Association) for 3 years and a board member for ten. In Palm Beach Gardens, Florida she sits on the board of the John E. Upledger Foundation, an international healthcare resource center recognized world wide for its comprehensive education programs, advanced treatment options, and unique outreach initiatives. She was also president of the Juno Beach Chapter of the Florida Shore and Beach Association- a key player in the restoration of the beaches, and a major part of the restoration of the first beach renourishment in the early 1990s. She has been active in numerous charities, and has served as chairperson for many charitable events.

Her past hobbies have included being an avid gardener, gourmet cook, and investor, but her primary interest has been her family. She and her husband reside in Juno Beach, Florida and Asheville, North Carolina, with their cat, Jackson

You can visit her website: www.maryjeanteachman.com

or

www.neversayinggoodbye.com